THE SENSE OF GLORY

The Sense of Glory
ESSAYS
IN CRITICISM

BY

HERBERT READ

Wer das Tiefste gedacht, liebt das Lebendigste
HÖLDERLIN

Essay Index Reprint Series

BOOKS FOR LIBRARIES PRESS, INC.
FREEPORT, NEW YORK

First Published 1930
Reprinted 1967

LIBRARY OF CONGRESS CATALOG CARD NUMBER: 67-26773

B·L·R

QVI
HIC ET UBIQVE
ALIT
GLORIAE SENSVM

Séparées en leurs applications spéciales, souvent opposées, ennemies même, les maîtrises diverses du monde des esprits se rencontrent sur les sommets où elles aspirent. La paix n'habite que les hauteurs. C'est en montant, montant toujours, que la lutte devient harmonie, et que l'apparente incohérence des efforts de l'homme aboutit à cette grande lumière, la gloire, qui est encore, quoi que l'on dise, ce qui a le plus de chance de n'être pas tout à fait une vanité... La gloire est quelque chose d'homogène et d'identique. Tout ce qui vibre la produit. Il n'y a pas plusieurs espèces de gloire, pas plus il n'y a plusieurs espèces de lumière. A un degré inférieur, il y a les mérites divers; mais la gloire de Descartes, celle de Pascal, celle de Molière, sont composées des mêmes rayons.

ERNEST RENAN, *Discours de Réception à l'Académie Française*
(3 Avril, 1879)

NOTE

THESE essays have appeared at intervals during the last four years in *The Times Literary Supplement*. With the permission of the Editor they are now, after some revision, published under a title that indicates their common theme.

The sense of glory is perhaps a phrase that has grown stale on our lips, and it may be a vain ambition of mine to attempt to reanimate it. As my excuse, I might repeat a saying of Renan's which Matthew Arnold once quoted: "Glory after all is the thing which has the best chance of not being altogether vanity." Glory may be only one form of romanticism; but so is every kind of idealism. Romanticism, whether we like it or not, is always with us. But though we cannot escape from romanticism, we can discriminate between the multiplicity of sentiments to which it gives rise, introducing among those sentiments an order whose integrity is this very sense of glory.

H. R.

CONTENTS

�֍

FROISSART

✦

FROISSART

Sir john froissart wrote his *Chronicles* at
the very end of the Middle Ages, and in this fact
more than any other lies their particular interest.
Froissart is the last witness to the life of an epoch,
and he wrote conscious of the fullness of that epoch
—conscious, one might think, almost of its dis-
integration. There is something foreboding in the
way this eager little man (there is perhaps no evidence for his littleness, nor yet for his leanness, but
a man so active in body and lively in observation
suggests the figure) ran up and down Europe in
quest of news, anxious to be on the scene of great
events, or at least to meet and interview, incon-
tinently, notebook in hand, those who had taken
part in these events. "Sa nature vive, mobile,
toujours *à la fenêtre*", is Sainte-Beuve's excellent
phrase for Froissart's qualities. We get a very good
picture of his methods in the first chapter of his
Third Book (the twenty-first chapter of the second
volume of Lord Berners' translation). Towards the
end of his previous book he had been taken up
with matters concerning the history of his own
country, Flanders, ending with the Peace of
Ghent, 1385.

"Then", writes Froissart, "seeing the peace was
made between the duke [of Burgundy] and them

of Gaunt, and it greatly annoyed me to be idle,
for I knew well that after my death this noble
and high history should have his course, wherein
divers noble men should have great pleasure and
delight, and as yet, I thank God, I have understanding and remembrance of all things past, and
my wit quick and sharp enough to conceive all
things shewed unto me touching my principal
matter, and my body as yet able to endure and
to suffer pain; all things considered, I thought
I would not let to pursue my said first purpose:
and to the intent to know the truth of deeds done
in far countries, I found occasion to go to the high
and mighty prince Gaston earl of Foix and of
Bearn: for I knew well that if I might have that
grace to come into his house and to be there at
leisure, I could not be so well informed to my
purpose in none other place of the world; for
thither resorted all manner of knights and strange
squires, for the great nobleness of the said earl.
And as I imagined, so I did, and shewed to my
redoubted lord the earl of Blois mine intent, and
he gave me letters of recommendations to the earl
of Foix. And so long I rode without peril or
damage, that I came to his house called Orthez
in the country of Bearn on Saint Katherine's day
the year of grace one thousand three hundred four-
score and eight. And the said earl, as soon as he

saw me, he made me good cheer and smiling said how he knew me, and yet he never saw me before, but he had often heard speaking of me; and so he retained me in his house to my great ease with the help of the letters of credence that I brought unto him, so that I might tarry there at my pleasure; and there I was informed of the business of the realms of Castile, Portugal, Navarre and Aragon, yea, and of the realm of England and country of Bourbonnois and Gascoyne. And the earl himself, if I did demand anything of him, he did shew me all that he knew, saying to me how the history that I had begun should hereafter be more praised than any other; and the reason, he said, why, was this, how that fifty year past there had been done more marvellous deeds of arms in the world than in three hundred year before that. Thus was I in the court of the earl of Foix well cherished and at my pleasure: it was the thing that I most desired to know news as touching my matter, and I had at my will lords, knights, and squires ever to inform me, and also the gentle earl himself."[1]

I have quoted this passage, not only because it shows Froissart in action, but also because there

[1] My quotations are taken in general from the Globe edition of Berners' Froissart, but I have also consulted the recent reprint of the full text published by the Shakespeare Head Press.

are phrases which reveal his clear consciousness of the splendour of the age whose deeds he was destined to record, as well as the high conception he had of his own function in recording them. "For I knew well that after my death this noble and high history should have his course" (*sera en grand cours* is the original, not quite exactly rendered by Berners)—we have no inclination to challenge this confident prophecy, still less inclination to question his claim to the understanding and remembrance of all things past, and to a wit quick and sharp enough (*esprit clair et aigu*) "to conceive all things shewed unto me". Froissart knew that he lived in a great age; did not Gaston de Foix, an earl "in everything so perfect that he cannot be praised too much", believe "how that fifty year past there had been done more marvellous deeds of arms in the world than in three hundred year before that"? "Three hundred year before that" comprised the whole age of chivalry, and now for fifty years, the fifty years covered by the chronicle Froissart had already written, that age had enjoyed a settled glory. That was one consideration; further, in an age when few men were capable of writing chronicles, and those few inevitably known to each other, it was safe to conclude that he, Sir John Froissart, was, by the grace of God, destined to be the only contemporary chronicler of this marvellous age; the age and the chronicle were henceforth one inseparable glory.

Froissart in England means the Froissart of Lord Berners' version, made about a century and a half after the writing of the original. We lose little in our dependence on this translation; it is often inaccurate and obscure; it is full of omissions and paraphrases; nevertheless, it has the spirit and the style of Froissart's French—"belle, facile et abondante". As the late W. P. Ker said in his introduction to the reprint of Berners in the Tudor Translations Series:

"It corresponds to the vocabulary of Froissart, the beauty of which, as of all good French, and not least in the French medieval prose, lies in the harmony between the single words and the syntactic idiom. The prose is not a new invention; it is natural, in the sense that it is founded upon the usages of conversation, quick and expressive, well provided with plenty of words for interesting things, unimpeded by drawling rhetoric, and free from any anxiety or curiosity about rules of good taste, because it had good taste to begin with, and did not need to think about it."[1]

This description of the qualities of French medieval prose could not be improved on; it is,

[1] *Essays on Medieval Literature*, 1905, pp. 152–3.

however, possible to pass beyond such an analysis and find a parallel between the qualities of this prose style and the characteristics of the age in general. The prose style was direct because the chronicler did not interpose his personality between the actuality of the event and the expression of it in narrative. 'Personality' in this sense was, indeed, a creation of the Renaissance, and if we want to see its presence clouding the clear stream of prose, we need only turn to Lord Berners' own prefaces written at the very zenith of that period. The diction there is just as involute and contorted as in Froissart it is simple. 'Personality' is perhaps not the word to press in this connection: it has never been properly defined; but to what else, but a consciousness of self, and to an expansive desire to enlarge the impression of one's personal grandeur, can we ascribe this practice of using three words where one would do, and of generally substituting the ornate for the simple, and a multiplicity for a unity? It is dangerous to seek comparisons in other arts, but if we are careful to select parallel environments, then we may trace something like the same difference between the poetry of Chaucer and that of Spenser, between the architecture of Coucy and that of Chambord, and so on, down to the costume, armour and all minor arts of these periods. In short, there is an essential difference, as between these periods, in the very way in which things are shaped in the human mind—or rather, in the way the human mind takes shape in things; and since our present tendency is away from the ornate, we cannot help having a decided sympathy for the form (as distinct from the content) of the art of the Middle Ages. Certainly, in the matter of prose style there is more essential similarity between Joinville and Froissart and the best modern narrative styles than between Froissart and the writers of any intervening age.

We began by saying that the main relevance of Froissart is that he was the best of all reporters of the pre-humanistic ideal of life; we see, therefore, in the first place that in the very act of reporting the life of his age, Froissart accomplished an art of prose which we might well desire to emulate. There is in all vigorous styles a direct reliance on an immediate observation of natural fact. This is the instinctive method of all epics, and we cannot open the Bible, or the *Iliad*, or the *Edda*, or the *Song of Roland*, without at once meeting these realistic images. There is nothing in human utterance to rival the emotional force of such vivid and elemental poetry, and though the words 'genius' and 'inspiration' may spring to our tongues ready to give an easy explanation of these magnifi-

cent virtues, we are baulked by the lack of any
definite individual with whom to invest such
qualities: the virtue of these epics is inseparable
from their anonymity. That is a theme we must
not pursue at present, but the bare mention of
it is sufficient to warn us that when we come to
an individual like Froissart, we must be careful
not to ascribe to his individuality what belongs
to his age. We can give full credit·to his understanding, and to his wit quick and sharp enough to
conceive all things shown unto him; these, however, have been the characteristics of good his-
torians in all ages. But only in the heroic ages do
these virtues conduce to a vivid and simple style,
for the heroic ages are the only ages in which men
live in daily contact with nature; at other times
they shut themselves up in courts and corridors,
and instead of force give us wit.

Froissart's chronicle is not an epic; a chronicle
is only the raw material of an epic. There is a
time element in the laws governing the formation
of an epic: it demands distance in memory and
perspective in design; it needs more than an individual point of view. As the story passes from
one generation to another, it becomes more definite, more compact; what is not apt for memory
gets forgotten. What remains is the eternally
significant. The virtue of a chronicle, however,

lies as much in its digressions as in its main theme;
there are long passages in Froissart that have epic
grandeur—we shall refer to them presently; there
are others, like the story of the lord of Corasse
and his familiar spirit Orthon, which are as fan-
tastic as any fairy-tale; and there are many others,
for the most part detailed accounts of manœuvres
and campaigning, which are as tedious as the
desiccated histories to which schoolboys are condemned. But the characteristic virtue of the
chronicle is just in its digressions; here it takes on
its particular vividness. In the following incident,
which has all the qualities of a good story of
adventure—speed, suspense, visibility—it is the
incidental details that shine out significantly: the
varlet's cloak, the poor hall 'black with smoke',
the small plancher and a ladder of 'seven steps',
a poor woman seated by a fire with a child in her
arms, and her ready answer to the rutters of
Ghent: "I went out right now and cast out a little
water and did close my door again."

"And when the earl heard those tidings, which
were right hard to him, as it was reason, he was
greatly then abashed and imagined what peril he
was in. Then he believed the counsel and would
go no farther, but to save himself if he might, and
so took his own counsel. He commanded to put
out all the lights, and said to them that were about

him: 'I see well there is no recovery: let every man depart and save himself as well he may.' And as he commanded it was done. The lights were quenched and cast into the streets, and so every man departed. The earl then went into a back lane and made a varlet of his to unarm him, and did cast away his armour, and put on an old cloak of his varlet's, and then said to him: 'Go thy way from me and save thyself if thou canst; and have a good tongue, an thou fall in the hands of thine enemies, and if they ask thee anything of me, be not beknown that I am in the town.' He answered and said: 'Sir, to die therefor I will speak no word of you.' Thus abode there the earl of Flanders all alone. . . .

"Thus about the hour of midnight the earl went from street to street and by back lanes, so that at last he was fain to take an house, or else he had been found by them of Gaunt. And so, as he went about the town, he entered into a poor woman's house, the which was not meet for such a lord. There was nother hall, palace nor chamber; it was but a poor smoky house. There was nothing but a poor hall, black with smoke, and above a small plancher and a ladder of seven steps to mount upon. And on the plancher there was a poor couch, whereas the poor woman's children lay. Then the earl, sore abashed and trembling, at his entering said: 'O good woman, save me: I am thy lord the earl of Flanders. But now I must hide me, for mine enemies chase me, and if ye do me good now, I shall reward you hereafter therefor.' The poor woman knew him well, for she had been oftentimes at his gate to fetch alms, and had often seen him as he went in and out a-sporting. And so incontinent, as hap was, she answered. For if she had made any delay, he had been taken talking with her by the fire. Then she said: 'Sir, mount up this ladder, and lay yourself under the bed that ye find, thereas my children sleep.' And so in the mean time the woman sate down by the fire with another child that she had in her arms. So the earl mounted up the plancher as well he might, and crept in between the couch and the straw and lay as flat as he could. And even therewith some of the rutters of Gaunt entered into the same house, for some of them said how they had seen a man enter into the house before them. And so they found the woman sitting by the fire with her child. Then they said: 'Good woman, where is the man that we saw enter before us into this house, and did shut the door after him?' 'Sirs', quoth she, 'I saw no man enter into this house this night. I went out right now and cast out a little water and did close my door again. If any were here, I could not tell

how to hide him. Ye see all the easement that
I have in this house. Here ye may see my bed,
and here above this plancher lieth my poor
children.' Then one of them took a candle and
mounted up the ladder and put his head above the
plancher, and saw there none other thing but the
poor couch where her children lay and slept. And
so he looked and then said to his company: 'Go
we hence; we lose the more for the less: the poor
woman saith truth; here is no creature but she
and her children.' And then they departed out
of the house. After that there was none entered
to do any hurt. All these words the earl heard
right well, whereas he lay under the poor couch."
(Vol. I, chap. cccc.)

This long passage does sufficient justice to the
literary qualities of Froissart, as reflected in Lord
Berners' good English. Had Froissart depended
solely on his merits as a master of prose narrative,
his reputation in France might have been greater
than it is. As a historian he has perhaps suffered
a little from the nationalistic prejudices of his
readers. Froissart was not a Frenchman; he was
a native of Valenciennes in Hainault. Philippa
of Hainault was Queen of England, and undoubtedly English interests and English affairs loomed
more largely in Froissart's understanding for that
very reason. On the other hand, Froissart had

exceptional knowledge of England, and of English life and character. He came to England in 1361 to present a book of his to Queen Philippa, and stayed some five years at the English Court. He travelled "nigh over all the realm of Scotland". He paid a second visit to England before the Queen's death in 1369, and came still again in 1394-5. It is doubtful whether nationalist sentiment was anywhere very strong in the Middle Ages; a stronger sentiment was devotion to a particular prince: the link was direct and tangible, person to person; not an abstract sentiment like patriotism. The nationality of Froissart himself is never very evident; that is part of his strength, for impartiality in the historian is not only the essential virtue of the craft; it is also the quality that endows history with one of the attributes of a universal art.

Sainte-Beuve, at any rate, has done justice to Froissart, calling his chronicle the book of honour, the bible of chivalry. It is still worth while insisting on this aspect. The philosophy of the Middle Ages is open for anyone to read; the *Summa* of St Thomas Aquinas is a complete guide to the intellectual life of the epoch, and the ways of its imaginative life can be traced in the *Divine Comedy*. But the contemporary life of action, out of which the intellect and the imagination were fed, is more obscure. Of the records that do exist, the great chronicles of Villehardouin, Joinville and Froissart are incomparably the most complete. Villehardouin and Joinville have their special virtues; but if only because he comes last and records most, Froissart is the most illuminating.

It is often held against the chroniclers that they were interested exclusively in the war-lords of their day, and had no thought for the common people. This complaint is rooted in a curious prejudice. Because the common people, including the burgesses who only became segregated into a class in a later age, have come to assume so important a function in the democratic state, it is assumed that the same class must have had an important function in the feudal age. As drawers of water and hewers of wood, no doubt they were essential to the economy of the country; but their status was actually that of serfdom, and to betray any particular interest in their social life is merely a backward reflection of modern humanitarian sentiment. The main stream of history in the Middle Ages passed them over; neither by virtue of economic function nor for their social significance do they deserve more attention than they actually get in a chronicle like Froissart's. They actually get a good deal. In the passage already quoted we have an intimate picture of a domestic interior. In his account of the Jacquerie revolt of 1357, and especially in the long detailed narrative devoted to Wat Tyler's insurrection, Froissart shows how ready he was to desert the chivalrous exploits of his knights to relate the history of the common people should their activities raise them out of the insignificance of serfdom. The whole story of Wat Tyler is told with such dramatic vividness that it is surprising it has not become the familiar possession of every English household. It is true that Froissart is too impartial to take a very favourable view of the rebels; they were 'ungracious' in themselves and their leaders were 'foolish'. But he presents their case with fairness and in detail, from the very words which John Ball used to preach in the cloister of Canterbury, to the final scene when the insolent behaviour of Wat Tyler in the presence of King Richard cost him his life.

Froissart might easily have taken this opportunity to contrast the characters of Wat Tyler and the boy king, the latter so fearless and capable on this occasion; but it is not part of a chronicler's business to point the moral; or perhaps Froissart takes his own code of values for granted. But at the end of his account of the Peasants' Revolt there is a paragraph about a certain knight, Sir Guichard d'Angle, which is

interesting because it gives us a summary list of
such values:

"And the same season there died in London a
knight called sir Guichard d'Angle, earl of Hun-
tingdon and master to the king. He was reverently
buried in the Friars preachers in London. And
on the day of his obsequy there was the king, his
two brethren, the princess his mother, and a great
number of prelates, barons and ladies of England,
and there did him great honour. And truly this
gentle knight was well worthy to have honour;
for in his time he had all noble virtues that a
knight ought to have. He was merry, true,
amorous, sage, secret, large, prewe, hardy, adventurous and chivalrous."

Such are the ten virtues of the medieval knight;
the words are well chosen by Froissart, and each
indicates an aspect of secular grace. Unfortu-
nately some of these words have lost their meaning;
the virtue, we might say, has gone out of them.
How degraded the word 'merry' has become;
the word 'prewe' (*preux*) we have lost altogether; and we are not to be trusted with the word
'amorous'. How Froissart understood some of
these words is well shown in his account of Gaston
de Foix:

"This earl Gaston of Foix, with whom I was,
at that time he was of a fifty year of age and nine;

and I say I have in my time seen many knights, kings, princes and other, but I never saw none like him of personage, nor of so fair form nor so well made. His visage fair, sanguine and smiling, his eyen gay and amorous, whereas he list to set his regard: in every thing he was so perfect that he cannot be praised too much. He loved that ought to be beloved, and hated that ought to be hated. He was a wise knight of high enterprise and of good counsel: he never had miscreant with him: he said many orisons every day, a nocturne of the psalter, matins of our Lady, of the Holy Ghost, and of the cross, and dirige. Every day he gave five florins in small money at his gate to poor folks for the love of God. He was large and courteous in gifts: he could right well take where it pertained to him and to deliver again whereas he ought. He loved hounds of all beasts; winter and summer he loved hunting. He never loved folly outrage nor folly largess; every month he would know what he spent: he took in his country, to receive his revenues and to serve him, notable persons, that is to say twelve receivers, and ever from two months to two months two of them should serve for his receipt; for at the two months' end he would change and put other two into that office, and one that he trusted best should be his controller, and to him all other should account, and the controller should account to him by rolls and books written, and the accounts to remain still with the earl. He had certain coffers in his chamber, out of the which he would ofttimes take money to give to lords, knights and squires, such as came to him, for none should depart from him without some gift; and yet daily multiplied his treasure to resist the adventures and fortunes that he doubted. He was of good and easy acquaintance with every man and amorously would speak to them. He was short in counsels and answers. He had four secretaries, and at his rising they must ever be ready at his hand without any calling, and when any letter were delivered him and that he had read it, then he would call them to write again, or else for some other thing.

"In this estate the earl of Foix lived; and at midnight when he came out of his chamber into the hall to supper, he had ever before him twelve torches brenning, borne by twelve varlets standing before his table at supper. They gave a great light, and the hall ever full of knights and squires, and many other tables dressed to sup who would. There was none should speak to him at his table, but if he were called. His meat was lightly wild fowl, the legs and wings all only, and in the day he did but little eat and drink. He had great

pleasure in harmony of instruments: he could do
it right well himself: he would have songs sung
before him. He would see conceits and fantasies
at his table, and when he had seen it, then he
would send it to the other tables.

"Briefly all this I considered and advised; and
or I came to his court, I had been in many courts
of kings, dukes, princes, earls and great ladies,
but I was never in none that so well liked me,
nor there was none more rejoiced (in) deeds of
arms than the earl did: there was seen in his hall,
chamber and court, knights and squires of honour
going up and down and talking of arms and of
amours: all honour there was found, all manner
of tidings of every realm and country there might
be heard, for out of every country there was resort
for the valiantness of this earl." (Vol. II, chap. xxvi.)

The story that follows, of the manner in which
Gaston the earl's son died, is not so agreeable for
our modern susceptibilities. The earl had refused
to stand surety for fifty thousand marks to his
brother-in-law, the king of Navarre. His wife had
thereupon deserted him, and gone to live at her
brother's court. Some years later, when Gaston
the earl's son was fifteen or sixteen years old, he
was allowed to go into Navarre to see his mother.
When he was ready to return, the king of Navarre
gave him a little purse of powder, instructing him

to keep it secret, but on some favourable opportunity to put some of the powder in his father's food—the purpose being "that your father should love again your mother". Gaston kept the purse concealed under his clothes, but he could not hide it from his bastard brother Yvain, with whom he slept. One day Gaston and Yvain "fell out together playing at tennis", and Gaston struck Yvain, "and the child went into his father's chamber and wept". He then told the earl about the purse of powder that Gaston wore concealed at his breast, and the earl told him to say nothing. But that night at dinner he called Gaston to him, discovered the purse and took it from him. He spread some of the powder on a trencher of bread and gave it to a dog; "and as soon as the dog had eaten the first morsel, he turned his eyen in his head and died incontinent". When the earl saw this, he took a knife and would have slain his son there and then, had not his knights and squires restrained him and beseeched him to make enquiry into the matter first. The child was thrown into a dark chamber, where he stayed ten days and refused to eat, "and he argued in himself and was full of melancholy and cursed the time that ever he was born and engendered, to come to such an end". Meanwhile the earl took fifteen of the squires that served his son, and on the mere suspicion that they had been cognisant of Gaston's secret, put them to death "right horribly"— "whereof", says Froissart, "it was great pity, for some of them were as fresh and as jolly squires as were any in the whole country, for ever the earl was served with good men". Then it was reported to the earl that his son was starving, so the earl went to visit him; "and in an evil hour he had the same time a little knife in his hand to pare withal his nails. He opened the prison door and came to his son and had the little knife in his hand not an inch out of his hand, and in great displeasure he thrust his hand to his son's throat, and the point of the knife a little entered into his throat into a certain vein, and said: 'Ah, traitor, why dost thou not eat thy meat?' and therewith the earl departed without any more doing or saying and went into his own chamber. The child was abashed and afraid of the coming of his father and also was feeble of fasting, and the point of the knife a little entered into a vein of his throat, and so fell down suddenly and died". The subsequent remorse of the earl does not blind us to the essential cruelty of his conduct. We cannot ignore, in fact, throughout the whole of these chronicles, the presence of what we should call a certain inhumanity. Human life was not valued highly; it was not respected as a sacred possession of the

individual, coming before all other values. But
before we condemn the Middle Ages for this harsh
characteristic, there are several questions we might
ask ourselves. We might ask: how firmly have we
ourselves eradicated man's inhumanity to man?
With ten million dead still fresh in the soil of
our battlefields, we can have no confident answer
to that question; "they died horribly". There are
many pettier cruelties of modern life which we
might mention; but let us pass on to a more importunate question: are the positive ideals, which
involve us in a righteous condemnation of the
inhumanity of the Middle Ages, so much more
admirable than the ideals which implied that
inhumanity? More concisely, are we sure that
the ideals of humanism are in any way more
admirable than the ideals of chivalry?

Humanism, which in spite of its many aspects
has remained a coherent tradition since the Renaissance, can be defined in many ways, but
perhaps its consistency can be reduced to an
essential belief in one dogma: the self-sufficiency
of natural man—the belief that the only values
that matter are human values. I describe this
attitude as a belief, but most people would call
it a fact. The late T. E. Hulme, in his essay on
"Humanism and the Religious Attitude" (*Specu-
lations*, 1924), pointed out the great significance of

doctrines which are thought of, not as doctrines, but as *facts*. "There are certain doctrines which for a particular period seem not doctrines, but inevitable categories of the human mind. Men do not look upon them merely as correct opinion, for they have become so much a part of the mind, and lie so far back, that they are never really conscious of them at all. They do not see them, but other things *through* them. It is these abstract ideas at the centre, the things which they take for granted, that characterize a period." Hulme's essay (it is hard to think of an essay which has done so much to clarify the ideas of a generation) is an attempt to distinguish the doctrinal facts of two periods, the Middle Ages and the Renaissance, the religious and the humanist periods. If, in reading medieval literature, particularly secular literature like the chronicles, we could always bear in mind this fundamental difference in the actual make-up of the world of 'facts', we should have a fairer comprehension of much that seems inhuman in the life of that time.

In the Middle Ages these 'facts' were, according to Hulme, "the belief in the subordination of man to certain absolute values, the radical imperfection of man, the doctrine of original sin. Everyone would assent to the assertion that these beliefs were held by the men of the Middle Ages. But that is not enough. It is necessary to realise that *these beliefs were the centre of their whole civilisation, and that even the character of their economic life was regulated by them*—in particular by the kind of ethics which springs from the acceptance of sin as a fact".

To read Froissart is an education in this truth. Everywhere there is evidence that life was indeed subordinate to certain absolute values. In the secular world, the lay world of knights and squires, such values are summed up in the word chivalry; and in Froissart's chronicle we have the supreme expression of these values. If Hulme made a mistake in his description of the ideology of the Middle Ages, it was in regarding it as exclusively religious. The ideals of chivalry and of Christianity are complementary rather than identical. The ideals of chivalry took shape under the same stress as the ideals of Christianity, but one was a philosophy of action, the other a philosophy of meditation. The knights of chivalry went on crusades to the Holy Land to rescue Christ's tomb from the hands of the infidel, but the spirit that inspired them was not specifically religious. Christ's tomb was the symbol of distress to be relieved, of honour to be redeemed. It was a cause, an oriflamme, a gage of glory. It differed only in degree from the gage of amour. It is impossible to deprive chivalry of its worldly trap-

pings, and why should we want to? Perhaps this
age was wise in thus keeping distinct the ideals of
the man of action and of the man of God.

At Poitiers, as the Black Prince rode and entered
in among his enemies, "he saw on his right hand
in a little bush lying dead the lord Robert of Duras
and his banner by him, and a ten or twelve of his
men about him. Then the prince said to two of his
squires and to three archers: 'Sirs, take the body of
this knight on a targe and bear him to Poitiers, and
present him from me to the cardinal of Perigord, and
say how I salute him by that token.' And this was
done. The prince was informed that the cardinal's
men were on the field against him, the which was
not pertaining to the right order of arms, for men
of the church that cometh and goeth for treaty
of peace ought not by reason to bear harness nor
to fight for neither of the parties; they ought to
be indifferent: and because these men had done
so, the prince was displeased with the cardinal,
and therefore he sent unto him his nephew the
lord Robert of Duras dead".

The cardinal of Perigord had been welcomed
before the battle as a mediator; he had travelled
freely from camp to camp, trying in vain to make
an honourable treaty between the prince and King
John of France. As a clerk he was regarded by
the prince as outside the strife of battle. The

presence of his retainers on the French side in the
battle could not be regarded as anything else but
base treachery. It was a confusion of spiritual
orders.

The Black Prince is the ideal man of action,
the ideal of chivalry, "courageous and cruel as a
lion". In his speech before the battle, the instinct
for action lies clearly distinguished by the side of
his true devotion to God; instinct and intelligence
are held jointly, but not confused:

"Now, sirs, though we be but a small company
as in regard to the puissance of our enemies, let
us not be abashed therefor; for the victory lieth
not in the multitude of people, but whereas God
will send it. If it fortune that the journey be ours,
we shall be the most honoured people of all the
world; and if we die in our right quarrel, I have
the king my father and brethren, and also ye have
good friends and kinsmen; these shall revenge us.
Therefore, sirs, for God's sake I require you to do
your devoirs this day; for if God be pleased and
Saint George, this day ye shall see me a good
knight."

God is with the right, but it is not for man to
presume to know which is the right. It is for man
to fight valiantly and chase his enemies. But the
passion and prejudice which endure when the
battle is over, were not known then. National

27

hatred held as a sentiment and independent of an objective sanction seems to be a consequence of that belief in man's self-sufficiency which I have taken as the characteristic of humanism. In the age of Froissart it was different; to fight cleanly meant to fight without rancour, and afterwards to treat your enemy with all the honour due to him under the code of chivalry. After the battle of Poitiers, when the French king was brought as a prisoner before the Black Prince, "the prince made lowly reverence to the king and caused wine and spices to be brought forth, and himself served the king in sign of great love". And furthermore:

"The same day of the battle at night the prince made a supper in his lodging to the French king and to the most part of the great lords that were prisoners. The prince made the king and his son, the lord James of Bourbon, the lord John d'Artois, the earl of Tancarville, the earl of Estampes, the earl Dammartin, the earl of Joinville and the lord of Partenay to sit all at one board, and other lords, knights and squires at other tables; and always the prince served before the king as humbly as he could, and would not sit at the king's board for any desire that the king could make, but he said he was not sufficient to sit at the table with so great a prince as the king was. But then he said to the king: 'Sir, for God's sake make none

28

evil nor heavy cheer, though God this day did not consent to follow your will; for, sir, surely the king my father shall bear you as much honour and amity as he may do, and shall accord with you so reasonably that ye shall ever be friends together after. And, sir, methink ye ought to rejoice, though the journey be not as ye would have had it, for this day ye have won the high renown of prowess and have passed this day in valiantness all other of your party. Sir, I say not this to mock you, for all that be on our party, that saw every man's deeds, are plainly accorded by true sentence to give you the prize and chaplet.' Therewith the Frenchmen began to murmur and said among themselves how the prince had spoken nobly, and that by all estimation he should prove a noble man, if God send him life and to persevere in such good fortune." (Vol. I, chap. clxviii.)

To distinguish between Chivalry and Christianity, between the man of action and the man of meditation, is not to lose sight of the primacy of spiritual values. The true knight was always devout. His occasional indifference to the man of God was part of that ethical realism implicit in the doctrine of original sin. No man is infallible. God is with the right. Let us put the matter to the test of our own valour, and whom God is with, will prevail.

The glory that men gained in this simple faith is the substance of Froissart's chronicle. The faith of men of action is perhaps always of this simple sort. The faith of men of meditation is more complex: it is more emotional. The fact that the chronicles are not concerned with this other faith does not mean that the chronicler was indifferent to its existence. Contemporary with Joinville, and the antitype of Froissart and all the medieval chronicles of action, is the *Golden Legend*, in which is recorded the fiercer glory of the saints. The *Summa* of St Thomas Aquinas, the *Golden Legend*, the *Divine Comedy* of Dante and Froissart's chronicle were all composed within about a hundred years. Together they represent the complex achievement of the Middle Ages, and individually they express the genius of that epoch in thought, word, deed, and in the love of God. Other epochs may have excelled the Middle Ages in the expression of one of these aspects of life; none has had the necessary virtue to combine them all in such splendour.

Froissart's pages are vivid with the personal radiance of men who achieve glory. There is no question here, as in Malory's case, of an author idealising a forgotten age. Froissart is the matter-of-fact reporter of events that happened in his own time, often under his own eyes. Naturally he was conscious of the glory of the deeds he recorded; but not as we are. For Froissart, glory was the measure of all things, the crown of all virtues. For us it has become something remote and elusive; even something romantic and literary. We have lost the sense of glory because we have lost the habit of faith. We neither love deeply enough, nor feel deeply enough, nor think deeply enough, to enjoy life's most impressive sanction.

❖

MALORY

❖

MALORY

THE *Morte Darthur*, like most of the books printed by Caxton, has had an influence on the course of English literature which it would be idle to estimate; and purely as literature Malory's 'miraculous' redaction has not wanted praise. 'Miraculous' was Professor Saintsbury's word, and is to be found in that *History of English Prose Rhythm* which paid such a notable tribute to Malory's originality and mastery in the formation of an English style. Professor Saintsbury did not by any means exhaust the technical virtues of Malory's prose; and now that the spirit of the age cries out for literature justified in action, for books visibly related to experience, we perceive more readily than ever certain subtleties of visual actuality and exact expression in the *Morte Darthur*. The last refinement of all great writing is the selection and isolation of significant detail; and no one is more triumphant in this sense than Malory. In the death scene of the Fair Maid of Astolat, for example, where for once English prose seems to out-reach the range of English verse, we see how a detail noted almost casually in the very last clause can inform the whole narrative with appropriate desolation and melancholy:

"And then she called her father, Sir Bernard,

and her brother, Sir Tirre, and heartily she prayed her father that her brother might write a letter like as she did indite it: and so her father granted her. And when the letter was written word by word like as she devised, then she prayed her father that she might be watched until she were dead. And while my body is hot let this letter be put in my right hand, and my hand bound fast with the letter until that I be cold; and let me be put in a fair bed with all the richest clothes that I have about me, and so let my bed and all my richest clothes be laid with me in a chariot unto the next place where Thames is; and let me be put within a barget, and but one man with me, such as ye trust to steer me thither, and that my barget be covered with black samite over and over; thus father I beseech you let it be done. So her father granted it her faithfully, all things should be done like as she had devised. Then her father and her brother made great dole, for when this was done anon she died. And so when she was dead the corpse and the bed all was led the next way unto Thames, and there a man, and the corpse, and all, were put unto Thames; and so the man steered the barget unto Westminster, and there he rowed a great while to and fro or any espied it."

In spite of these and other great merits, the

Morte Darthur is to-day in a curious predicament—
sometimes a butt for facetious scorn, sometimes a
hobby-horse for romanticists, and when it has
escaped these fates, a feast to be served in polite
selections to schoolgirls. It almost seems that
great books must be defamed before they can become popular; I have seen an emasculated edition
of *Gulliver's Travels* sold on the bookstalls as one
of a series of "Sunny Stories for Little Folks".
Malory's genius has not been travestied in market-
place and nursery in quite the same way as
Swift's; but certain perversions of the spirit of
his work have prevented the true appreciation of
its merits.

The first of these might be called the quixotic-
perversion. The *Morte Darthur* is really the epitome
of the literature of an age—the feudal age. It was
written at the break-up of that age by one who
shared in its stress and anguish with body and soul
—so at least we may conclude if, as now seems
likely, the author of the *Morte Darthur* can be identified with the Sir Thomas Malorie of Newbold
Revel, in the parish of Monks Kirby, Warwick-
shire, whose name occurs among those of a
number of Lancastrians excluded from a general
pardon granted by Edward IV in 1468. The turbulent career of this knight has been reconstructed
with a good deal of ingenuity by Mr Edward

Hicks.[1] Malory probably began his adventurous life as a member of the retinue of Richard Beauchamp, Earl of Warwick, and undoubtedly saw many years of active military service in France. Later in his life, in his native country, he became involved in adventures which we might really call 'quixotic', and was charged with insurrection, robbery and rape. He pleaded "in no wise guilty" of all these charges, but his plea was dismissed, and he seems to have spent the remaining twenty years of his life in prison; during that time he composed the *Morte Darthur*.

Malory was formulating for the last time a tradition which had lasted for five hundred years. He was writing of events remote enough to be legendary. The reaction was fast upon him, and when it came it fell foul of what was nearest and handiest—the *Morte Darthur*. The damosels and knights of the Arthurian cycle were fair objects and easy victims for the scorn of an age that had grown wealthy, realistic and cynical. The legendary charm lasted until Spenser, in whom, however, romance has become too ornate and sophistical; and in a more general and yet a more profound way the spirit of Malory is the spirit of the Elizabethans, particularly of that embodiment o

---

[1] *Sir Thomas Malory. His Turbulent Career.* A Biography by Edward Hicks. Harvard University Press, 1928.

all most remarkable in the age, Sir Philip Sidney. But the reaction, fed by a more diffuse and bourgeois spirit, came to a head in such travesties as *The Knight of the Burning Pestle*. The world has been pleased to see this mockery sanctioned in *Don Quixote*; but that is a superficial view of Cervantes' romance. No thoughtful reader ever came from *Don Quixote* in a cynic or ironic mood against the age of chivalry. Señor Unamuno[1] has made his great protest in this sense.

"They say that thy biography, my lord Don Quixote, was written to amuse, and to cure us of the folly of heroism; and they add that the fun-maker achieved his object. Thy name has come to be, for many, another name for mockery, a hocus-pocus to exorcize heroisms and belittle grandeurs. We shall not recover our manliness of yore until we resent the hoax in good earnest and play the Quixote with the greatest seriousness and uncompromisingly.

"Most readers of thy story, sublime madman, laugh at it; but they cannot profit by its spiritual content until they mourn over it. . . . In that jocular volume is the saddest story ever written; the saddest, yes, but the most consoling to those

[1] *The Life of Don Quixote and Sancho according to Miguel de Cervantes Saavedra.* Expounded with comment by Miguel de Unamuno. Translated by Homer P. Earle, 1928.

who can enjoy, through tears of delight, redemption from the wretched practicality to which our present mode of life condemns us."

No mockery of the human spirit, however irrational that spirit may be, ever survives the hour of its expression. *Don Quixote* was not a mockery, but an affirmation of chivalry and honour. Cervantes himself had no illusions left at the end of a hard life, but he knew that the sentiment of glory was no illusion, that nothing worthy was ever done that was not done for the sake of glory. But such an interpretation of Cervantes is not the obvious one; and what we will call a facile quixotism has prevailed, many fools facetiously mouthing phrases like "fair damsel in distress", "the goodly Knight that pricketh on the plain", and so on, for the few graceful spirits that penetrate this perverse screen of mockery to the great morality underlying it.

The second obstacle which a reader of the *Morte Darthur* must overcome is the romantic perversion. This is more difficult to avoid because ostensibly we are among friends. But Malory has had no greater enemies than his revivalists. *La Belle Dame Sans Merci* may pass as a momentary reincarnation of the magic of the *Morte Darthur*; but the travesties of Tennyson and Morris, followed by the effeminate and etiolated ornaments of Aubrey

Beardsley, have had disastrous effects. They bathe the stark narrative in an atmosphere of milk and honey; they turn romance into romanticism, muscular prose into watery verse. Such pretenders shrink from the vigorous realism of Malory. Tennyson regrets

> "One
> Touched by the adulterous finger of a time
> That hover'd between war and wantonness
> And crownings and dethronings",

and improves on Malory by making his Arthur a king of prigs. Even the noble simplicity of Malory's style is translated into the sentimentality of a Victorian valentine. Compare Elaine's last letter:

"Most noble knight, Sir Launcelot, now hath death made us two at debate for your love. I was your lover, that men called the Fair Maiden oi Astolat; therefore unto all ladies I make my moan, yet pray for my soul and bury me at least, and offer ye my mass-penny: this is my last request. And a clean maiden I died, I take God to witness: pray for my soul, Sir Launcelot, as thou art peerless."
—with Tennyson's versification of it:

> "Most noble lord, Sir Lancelot of the Lake,
> I, sometime call'd the maid of Astolat,
> Come, for you left me taking no farewell,
> Hither, to take my last farewell of you.

I loved you, and my love had no return,
And therefore my true love has been my death.
And therefore to our lady Guinevere,
And to all other ladies, I make moan.
Pray for my soul, and yield me burial.
Pray for my soul thou too, Sir Lancelot,
As thou art a knight peerless."

To romanticize and sentimentalize the *Morte Darthur* is to sacrifice its finest essence, which is action and intact honour displayed in the midst of all worldly perils—cowardice, murder, hate and sin.

The third obstacle to the modern appreciation of Malory is in the nature of a reaction from the perversion just mentioned. People sick of romantic transcriptions of chivalry turn away without investigating the thing itself. Anti-romantic as most of this generation must be, we imagine that all romance is romantic. It is a great error; and if the excuse is not ignorance, it is merely indifference. But an age with so few illusions, with such poor outlets for emotion and reverence, cannot afford to be either indifferent or ignorant, and must in the end go to Malory and his like to recover certain necessary virtues—virtues which Unamuno finds implicit in the figure of Don Quixote.

All such virtues are included in the sentiment of glory. It may seem odd that a generation which has lived to experience the bitterest disillusion of glory should be urged to recover that sentiment from an old romance. But glory itself has been perverted, for many centuries and from many causes. We need not be concerned with historical evidences; modern instances will suffice. The first of these is the combination of glory and nationalism, a fault from which we English can by no means hold ourselves free, though we leave to French writers like Barrès and Maurras the literary apologetics for such a misalliance. Nationalism is a deeply rooted instinct, and however irrational such instincts may be, they cannot be lightly dismissed by an appeal to absolute standards in the manner of M. Benda.[1] Nevertheless, it is necessary to affirm that absolute virtues cannot pertain to an arbitrary and delimited group of men; or to a cause that is less than human: virtue is universal, and glory, which is the radiance of virtue, is only gained through universal passions. But passions pertain to the individual, and universal virtues can only be pursued by the individual mind. Or as La Rochefoucauld observed: "Il est aussi honnête d'être glorieux avec soi-même qu'il

[1] See especially *La Trahison des Clercs* by this author, translated into English by Richard Aldington as *The Great Betrayal,* 1928.

42

est ridicule de l'être avec les autres." For such reasons the most notable appeal to glory made by a moralist in our time, that of Georges Sorel in *Reflections on Violence*, must be dismissed because it too turns a disinterested and individual force into a sanction for a particular faction. Sorel tried to graft on to the *idea* of proletarian revolt an *energy* which could and would achieve that idea; and he realized that the only adequate energy was a feeling for sublimity, a sense of glory. Successful tyrannies, as of a Lenin or a Mussolini, depend on the creation of such an enthusiasm, and are remarkable for nothing so much as the fact that they are individual triumphs, personal ideals maintained as much by the power of legendary inspiration as by deliberate force.

Glory has usually been associated with war, and in Malory is accompanied by what his first critic, Roger Ascham, called "bold bawdry and open manslaughter". That glory has no necessary connection with war is clear after a moment's reflection; for martial glory is not essential glory, and we must still distinguish glory with grace—as in Wolfe and Nelson—from glory with pride—as in Alexander and Napoleon. War occupies a privileged position because it alone has provided a large number of people with an opportunity for disinterested action. That is the burden of many apologies for war, such as those of Proudhon and Ruskin. War allows men to seek glory without pretension, in the shelter of a crowd, with the excuse of a common cause. As Vauvenargues pointed out in one of his maxims, the dominating qualities in men are not those which they willingly allow to appear, but, on the contrary, those which they hide. "This especially applies to ambition, because it is a kind of humiliating recognition of the superiority of great men, and an avowal of the meanness of our fortune or the presumption of our spirit. Only those who desire little, or those who are on the point of realizing their pretensions, can be openly complacent about such things. What makes people ridiculous is a sense of pretensions ill-founded or immoderate, and since glory and fortune are advantages most difficult to attain, they are for that reason the source of the deepest sense of ridicule in those who lack them." Vauvenargues, to whom I shall devote a later essay, has perhaps more to say of good sense on this subject than any other moralist; and because he himself was such a fine example of the pure love of glory, rather like our Sir Philip Sidney, we ought to pay special attention to his analysis. His two *Discours* expound the Greek conception of glory, and all he asks is that he may speak to his friend on this subject as he would have been able to speak to an Athenian of the time of Themistocles and of Socrates. Vauvenargues was writing in the eighteenth century in the full blast of La Rochefoucauld's cynicism, in an age whose prudent egotism found memorable expression in the verse of an English poet:

"The paths of glory lead but to the grave."

—a sentiment which Vauvenargues had anticipated and for which he provided the right retort:

"A la mort, dit-on, que sert la gloire? Je réponds: Que sert la fortune? que vaut la beauté? Les plaisirs et la vertu même ne finissent-ils pas avec la vie? La mort nous ravit nos honneurs, nos trésors, nos joies, nos délices, et rien ne nous suit au tombeau. Mais de là qu'osons-nous conclure? sur quoi fondons-nous nos discours? Le temps où nous ne serons plus est-il notre objet? Qu'importe au bonheur de la vie ce que nous pensons à la mort? Que peuvent, pour adoucir la mort, la mollesse, l'intempérance ou l'obscurité de la vie?"

How strange it is, he says, that we should have to incite men to glory and prove to them beforehand its advantages!

"Cette forte et noble passion, cette source ancienne et féconde des vertus humaines, qui a fait sortir le monde de la barbarie et porté les arts à leur perfection, maintenant n'est plus regardée

que comme une erreur imprudente et une écla-
tante folie. Les hommes se sont lassés de la vertu;
et, ne voulant plus qu'on les trouble dans leur
dépravation et leur mollesse, ils se plaignent que
la gloire se donne au crime hardi et heureux, et
n'orne jamais le mérite. Ils sont sur cela dans
l'erreur; et, quoi qu'il leur paraisse, le vice
n'obtient point d'hommage réel."

The *Discours* from which these passages are
quoted is a noble piece of eloquence, itself expressing the noblest attitude of mind. The essential
argument is that glory and virtue are interdepen-
dent; one cannot exist without the other. The
more virtue men have, the more they are entitled
to glory; and the nearer glory is to them, the more
they like it, the more they want it, the more they
feel its reality. But when virtue has degenerated;
when talent or strength is lacking; when levity and
ease govern all other passions—then glory seems
a long way off; you cannot count on it, or cultivate
it, so finally men come to regard it as a dream,
and ignore it. It is much better that we should
allow ourselves to be led astray by this sentiment.
What does it matter if we are deceived, since in
the process we gain talent, feeling, sensibility?
What does it matter if we never attain our end,
if on the way we gather such noble flowers, if even
in adversity our conscience is serener than that

of men merely viciously happy? We are reminded again of Unamuno, who expresses almost precisely similar thoughts in the book from which I have already quoted:

"Heroic or saintly life has always followed in the wake of glory, temporal or eternal, earthly or celestial. Believe not those who tell you they seek to do good for its own sake, without hope of reward; if that were true, their souls would be like bodies without weight, purely apparitional. To preserve and multiply the human race there was given us the instinct and sentiment of love between man and woman; to enrich it with grand deeds there was given us the thirst for glory."

Again and again these two authors, so typical of the spirit of their diverse countries, reinforce one another. In the *Introduction à la Connaissance de l'Esprit Humain* Vauvenargues speaks of this same sense of the ineluctability of glory:

"La gloire nous donne sur les cœurs une autorité naturelle qui nous touche sans doute autant que nulle de nos sensations, et nous étourdit plus sur nos misères qu'une vaine dissipation: elle est donc réelle en tous sens.

"Ceux qui parlent de son néant inévitable soutiendraient peut-être avec peine le mépris ouvert d'un seul homme. Le vide des grandes passions est rempli par le grand nombre des petites: les contempteurs de la gloire se piquent de bien danser, ou de quelque misère encore plus basse. Ils sont si aveugles qu'ils ne sentent pas que c'est la gloire qu'ils cherchent si curieusement, et si vains qu'ils osent la mettre dans les choses les plus frivoles. La gloire, disent-ils, n'est ni vertu, ni mérite; ils raisonnent bien en cela: elle n'est que leur récompense; mais elle nous excite donc au travail et à la vertu, et nous rend souvent estimables afin de nous faire estimer."

Vauvenargues then compares the love of glory with the love of knowledge. They are alike in principle, for both spring from a sense of our imperfection. But glory tries as it were to create a new being from without, the love of knowledge to extend and cultivate the being within.

The glory which Vauvenargues saw in the clear light of reason, and which Cervantes saw in the gentler light of a profound sympathy, Malory saw as the mainspring of action. Vauvenargues finds it necessary to defend glory; Cervantes must approach it obliquely, smother it in hocus-pocus; but Malory takes it as a matter of course: it is the natural thirst of all 'men of worship'. Worship ('worth-ship') is a word which recurs many times throughout the *Morte Darthur*; the glossaries usually give its meaning as 'honour', but from the context it is evident that it means something more definite.

It means active honour, magnanimity, *grandeur d'âme*, glory gained. The tale of Sir Gareth of Orkney "that was called Beaumains"—a part of the *Morte Darthur* which seems to be dependent to an unusual extent on Malory's own genius—illustrates the concept of worship more clearly than most of Malory's tales. Three men and a dwarf arrived at King Arthur's Court, and when they had alighted from their horses, "right so came into the hall two men well beseem and richly, and upon their shoulders there leaned the goodliest young man and the fairest that ever they all saw, and he was large and long, and broad in the shoulders, and well visaged, and the fairest and largest handed that ever man saw, but he fared as though he might not go nor bear himself but if he leaned upon their shoulders". This was Sir Gareth in disguise, and he asked of the King three gifts, one to be given then, and the other two on that day twelvemonth. The first request was that he should be given meat and drink for that twelvemonth. The King judged his man to be "of right great worship", and though the request surprised him, he did not refuse it. He handed the stranger over to his steward, Sir Kay, to be treated as though he were a lord's son. Subtleties of conduct and bearing were beyond Sir Kay, and he was for not treating the stranger so grandly, "for I dare undertake he is a villain born, and never will make man, for an he had come of gentlemen he would have asked of you horse and armour, but such as he is, so he asketh. And sithen he has no name, I shall give him a name that shall be Beaumains, that is ⸱⸱⸱ ⸱⸱nds, and into the kitchen I shall bring him, and ⸱here he shall have fat brose every day, that he s⸱ ⸱ll be as fat by the twelvemonth's end as a pork hog Sir Gawaine and Sir Launcelot protested against this treatment of one who they thought would prove "a man of great worship". "Beware, said Sir Launcelot, so ye gave the good knight Brewnor, Sir Dinadan's brother, a name, and ye called him La Cote Male Taile, and that turned you to anger afterward. As for that, said Sir Kay, this shall never prove none such. For Sir Brewnor desired ever worship, and this desireth bread and drink and broth; upon pain of my life he was fostered up in some abbey, and, howsomever it was, they failed meat and drink, and so hither he is come for his sustenance." And Sir Kay got his way; and Beaumains "set him down among boys and lads, and there he ate sadly". At the twelvemonth's end there came a damosel, asking for succour, but because she would not tell her name, the King would not allow any of his knights to go with her. Then Beaumains stepped forward and asked for the two gifts that had been promised him, and he asked that he should be granted this adventure of the damosel, and that he should be knighted by Sir Launcelot for this purpose. The King granted him these gifts, but "Fie on thee, said the damosel, shall I have none but one that is your kitchen page? Then was she wroth and took her horse and departed". After jousting with Sir Launcelot, and having obtained the order of knighthood, Beaumains set off in pursuit of the damosel, who received him with high spirit and undisguised scorn. Malory here shows his admirable sense of humour:

"When he had overtaken the damosel, anon she said, What dost thou here? Thou stinkest all of the kitchen, thy clothes be bawdy of the grease and tallow that thou gainest in King Arthur's kitchen; weenest thou, said she, that I allow thee, for yonder knight that thou killest. Nay truly, for thou slewest him unhappily and cowardly; therefore turn again, bawdy kitchen page, I know thee well, for Sir Kay named thee Beaumains. What art thou but a lusk and a turner of broaches and a ladle-washer? Damosel, said Beaumains, say to me what ye will, I will not go from you whatsomever ye say, for I have undertaken to King Arthur for to achieve your adventure, and so shall I finish it to the end, either I shall die therefore. Fie on thee,

kitchen knave, wilt thou finish mine adventure?
thou shalt anon be met withal, that thou wouldest
not for all the broth that ever thou suppest once
look him in the face. I shall assay, said Beaumains."

That quiet, confident reply takes us back once
more to Don Quixote, with his equally quiet and
confident "Yo sé quién soy". And Unamuno's
comment is once again apt for the English epic:

"In saying, 'I know who I am', Don Quixote
said only, 'I know what I will be!' That is the
hinge of all human life: to know what one wills
to be. Little ought you to care who you are; the
urgent thing is what you will to be. The being
that you are is but an unstable, perishable being,
which eats of the earth and which the earth some
day will eat; what you will to be is the idea of you
in God, the Consciousness of the universe; it is the
divine idea of which you are the manifestation in
time and space. And your longing impulse toward
the one you will to be, is only homesickness drawing you toward your divine home. Man is complete and upstanding only when he would be more
than man."

The subsequent adventures of Beaumains show
how, after many arduous encounters with ob-
streperous knights, he at last overcame the re-
pugnance of the damosel, whose name was Linet,
but not before an illuminating conversation had

taken place on the subject of 'worship'. After his fourth encounter, Sir Beaumains and the damosel set forth again, "and ever she rode chiding him in the foulest manner":

"Damosel, said Beaumains, ye are uncourteous so to rebuke me as ye do, for me seemeth I have done you good service, and ever ye threaten me I shall be beaten with knights that we meet, but ever for all your boast they lie in the dust or in the mire, and therefore I pray you rebuke me no more;—and when ye see me beaten or yielden as recreant, then may ye bid me go from you shamefully; but first I let you wit I will not depart from you, for I were worse than a fool an I would depart from you all the while that I win worship. Well, said she, right soon there shall meet a knight shall pay thee all thy wages, for he is the most man of worship of the world, except King Arthur. I will well, said Beaumains, the more he is of worship, the more shall be my worship to have ado with him."

It is easy now to identify Malory's 'worship' with Vauvenargues' and Unamuno's sentiment of glory. The further exploits of Beaumains show how he won greater worship, and how he rescued and wedded Dame Lionesse of the Castle Perilous. But one thing is to be observed as typical of this 'path of glory': each triumph is made to contribute to the greater glory of King Arthur, the defeated knights are one by one made to swear fealty to Beaumains' overlord. This, however, is not in any way to be interpreted as an abstraction of the sentiment of glory: the worship is definitely personal to Arthur himself. The King is a knight of knights, a great leader like Charlemagne, but not a symbol; king by the magic test of Excalibur, but not by divine right; king in virtue of his great worship only.

The mention of Charlemagne calls to mind the *Song of Roland*, which might well be named the 'Song of Worship', for in that great epic human glory shines out in pure masculine beauty. In this the *Song of Roland* is superior to the *Morte Darthur*, which pays as the price of its enhanced romance all the confusion and disaster of sexual passion. A militant religion is the mainspring of action in the *Song of Roland*, but the sense of glory is the individual sense. There is no suggestion of gaining glory for a particular body like Church or State; glory is pursued at the expense of flesh:

"Dieu! dit le Roi, que ma vie est peineuse!"

There is base treachery in the *Song of Roland*, but the *Morte Darthur* is dark with sexual intrigue. The morals, to an ascetic like Ascham, or to a conventionalist like Tennyson, could not appear as anything but queer. Malory himself excuses the adulterous conduct of Launcelot and Queen Guenever with the naïve remark: "For love that time was not as is nowadays". This makes all the more curious the last chapter of Book XVIII, with its lament for love in the old way. True love is compared to the month of May:

"For then all herbs and trees renew a man and woman, and likewise lovers call again to their mind old gentleness and old service, and many kind deeds that were forgotten by negligence. For like as winter rasure does always erase and deface green summer, so fareth it by unstable love in man and woman. For in many persons there is no stability; for we may see all day, for a little blast of winter's rasure, anon we shall deface and lay apart true love for little or nought, that cost much thing; this is no wisdom nor stability, but it is feebleness of nature and great disworship, whomsoever useth this. Therefore like as May month flowereth and flourisheth in many gardens, so in like wise let every man of worship flourish his heart in this world, first unto God, and next unto the joy of them that he promised his faith unto; for there was never worshipful man or worshipful woman, but they loved one better than another; and worship in arms may never be foiled, but first reserve the honour to God, and secondly the quarrel must come of thy lady; and such love I call virtuous love.

"But nowadays men can not love seven night, but they must have all their desires; that love may not endure by reason; for where they be soon accorded and hasty heat, soon it cooleth. Right so fareth love nowadays, soon hot soon cold; this is no stability. But the old love was not so; men and women could love together seven years, and no licours lusts were between them, and then was love, truth, and faithfulness; and lo, in like wise was used love in King Arthur's days."

Malory is here moralizing, and expressing his own spirit rather than the spirit of his narrative. He seeks, like Don Quixote, to identify love and glory. It was a paradox more evident to the age of Malory and of Cervantes (for theirs were essentially the same age) than to the legendary age in which Malory found the sources of his romance. We might say that in the interval the moral sense had become finer, that manners had improved, and that a code of honour had been established; we might say such things did not a deeper instinct tell us that mankind has always been the same in such matters, beneficent and cruel by turns, in love chaste and stable one day, harsh and adulterous the next; the true life being lived only by those who, like Sir Beaumains and Don Quixote, see beyond the futility of what is to the glory of what might be.

❖

DESCARTES

❖

DESCARTES

THE Abbé Baillet, in his life of Descartes, relates how one day in November, 1628, a small company was gathered together in the house of the Papal Nuncio, Guidi di Bagno, to listen to the discourse of a certain Sieur de Chandoux, who had a new philosophy which he wished to substitute for the outworn doctrines of scholasticism. Among the company were Descartes and the Cardinal de Bérulle, founder of the Congregation of the Oratory and a Catholic diplomat whose hand may be traced in many affairs of the first part of the seventeenth century. The Sieur de Chandoux was perhaps a charlatan; at any rate, he was later convicted and hanged on a charge of forging money, though it is just possible that his crime was no more than an indiscreet devotion to experimental chemistry. However that may be, it is certain that on the occasion of which we speak he made a brave show of eloquence and plausibility. Everyone there seemed to be carried away by his arguments —everyone except Descartes. He remained silent and, when de Bérulle invited him to express an opinion, made a pretence of modesty and unwillingness. But pressed by the Cardinal, he quickly but quietly demolished the feeble structure of Chandoux' neo-scholasticism. He did not, for the moment, enter upon an exposition of the new thoughts which had begun to ferment in his own mind; but he did indicate, at the end of his speech, his possession of a method whereby it would be possible to establish in philosophy certain principles so clear and indubitable that all the processes of nature would become explicable. The curiosity of the assembly was aroused, and de Bérulle went so far as to invite Descartes to pay him a visit so that the new method might be explained to him in more detail. Descartes was greatly flattered (for socially he was never lacking in a profound respect for those in authority), and a few days afterwards he had given to the Cardinal a more intimate account of his discovery.

The encounter was decisive for Descartes; it was a significant moment in the history of modern thought. De Bérulle was a great organizer; not only had he founded the Congregation of the Oratory, but just at this time was recruiting a new society, the Company of the Holy Sacrament, which was to be a vast army of devout Catholic laymen, mobilized for the struggle against Protestantism and free thought. For this organization he needed, above all, a corps of controversialists—men apt for the destruction of heresies and the demonstration of the true faith. In Descartes he immediately perceived his man; and there is no doubt that then and there a definite relationship was established between the two. M. Alfred Espinas, in the extremely interesting study which he has devoted to the development of Descartes' ideas,[1] would go farther and impute to de Bérulle a complete dominance over the conscience and practical activities of Descartes; and certainly Baillet implies as much. Nor is such a relationship in conflict with what else we know of Descartes' personality. It was a strange mixture of mental acuteness and natural piety; and it is really in the persistence of these two strains that we must seek for an explanation of the enormous paradox of his philosophy.

Baillet tells us that Descartes looked on M. de Bérulle as, after God, "le principal auteur de ses desseins et de sa retraite hors de son pays". Descartes' life becomes settled from this moment. He retired to Holland to escape the importunate society of his countrymen, and there set about, deliberately and solemnly, to execute the great task with which he had been entrusted, which was to apply his infallible method to the sphere of natural theology.

"'The Cardinal', says Baillet, 'was not slow to see the importance of the project, and judging

[1] *Descartes et la Morale* (Études sur l'Histoire de la Philosophie de l'Action). By Alfred Espinas. Two volumes. Paris, 1925.

Descartes as very capable of carrying it out, used the authority which he possessed over his mind to persuade him to undertake this great work. He even put it to him as an obligation of conscience, in that having received from God an ability and insight in these matters not accorded to others, he should render to Him an exact account of the use of his talents, and should be responsible to this sovereign judge of men for the wrong he would do to mankind should he deprive them of the fruit of his meditations. He went so far as to assure Descartes that with such pure intentions, and with such a wide intelligence as he knew him to have, God would not fail to bless his work and to crown it with all possible success.'"

From the Cardinal de Bérulle to M. Jacques Maritain[1] is not so long a step as might appear. M. Maritain would have made an admirable auxiliary for the 'Cabale des Dévots' (as the Company of the Holy Sacrament was called by its adversaries). He is the great lay-apologist for the neo-Catholics in France to-day. His published works are already considerable in number, and not negligible in force and cogency. They include a long and careful examination of the philosophy of Bergson, a criticism of the basis of the modern

---

[1] *Trois Réformateurs: Luther, Descartes, Rousseau.* By Jacques Maritain. Paris, 1926.

theory of knowledge (*Réflexions sur l'Intelligence*) and various essays on those aspects of modern life and literature which bring most into question the nature of our own beliefs. He is an eager and active controversialist, and exercises a considerable influence on contemporary French writers—an influence that sometimes reveals itself in most unexpected quarters. It gives us, then, a measure of the immense divagation that somehow or other was caused by this innocent enterprise of Descartes to find him ranged with Luther and Rousseau as the inspiration of that modernity to which M. Maritain addresses his hostile rhetoric. Of the innocency of Descartes there can be no doubt. His recently discovered correspondence with Constantyn Huygens[1] reveals him in his retirement preoccupied with the avocations, not of an heresiarch, but of a God-fearing student whose only desire is to have liberty to pursue his studies. This correspondence is the record of a perfect intellectual friendship, and the revelation of a mind in all things serene, considerate and earnest. His faith is secure, his spirit unperturbed; only the intelligence is busy, probing into the mechanism so carefully dissociated from the being of God. But he worked among unseen springs and endless reverberations.

[1] *Correspondence of Descartes and Constantyn Huygens*, 1635–47. Edited by Leon Roth. Clarendon Press, 1926.

The doubts dismissed from his own mind were not so easily dislodged from places where the prior faith was lacking.

From the first the new method gave rise to anxieties, but its success was never in doubt. The history of modern philosophy is a history of the development of Cartesianism in its dual aspect of idealism and mechanism. Only within recent years has that triumphant progress been checked. The manifold errors of the system have always been obvious and freely criticized. But only now have we begun to realize how totally wrong are its very first assumptions; only now have we begun to see in this simple and direct philosophy the source of all the great intellectual sophisms of our age.

This fatal criticism comes from two quite different camps; it is a corollary of the most recent advances of science, and it is a doctrine of that revival of scholasticism represented in France by M. Maritain. It would be interesting to inquire how far these two quite different schools of thought coincide—how near, that is to say, they approach each other in their metaphysical assumptions. Their terminology might well be quite different, one being derived from an ancient tradition, the other from a new science, and it is very hard to strip a system of thought of its slowly evolved mode of expression. But if, on further research, it appears that the differences of religion (of *a* religion, it is true) and of science are merely logical, differences of mode rather than of mood, then the situation becomes tremendously significant. Obviously we exist, as an age or an epoch, in a state of indecision; the easy assumption is that we exist in a state of despair. But the facts equally suggest that we may be on the boundaries of a new life. The modern atmosphere is much the same as that in which the party met three hundred years ago in the *salon* of Guidi di Bagno. There is the same condition of stalemate, the same agitation of minds, all eager for a new light. And it is not difficult to find protagonists who would fit the rôles of the Sieur de Chandoux and Descartes; perhaps M. Maritain would do for one and Professor Whitehead for the other—though which for which is difficult to determine. Only it should be noted that on that famous occasion Descartes confessed to a whole-hearted sympathy with the aims of de Chandoux: he merely begged to offer a different— a more infallible—method of procedure.

To bring the Abbé Baillet's ingenuous account of Descartes' departure to his philosophical retreat, there to renovate the natural theology of the Church, into opposition with M. Maritain's bitter and ably destructive analysis of that renovation, perhaps savours of ironic facility. But it is the irony of events. M. Maritain goes so far as to say that the Cartesian reform is the one great sin committed by the French in the history of modern thought. Its devout originator, who believed in nothing so much as the goodness of God, who was passionately attached to the practice of his religion, and who, even in the act of formulating his philosophy, made a pilgrimage to Loretto—by what strange chance has this man come to assume the satanic dignity accorded to him by a modern Catholic? It is only done, of course, by strictly dissociating the philosopher from his philosophy; and this M. Maritain makes his first task:

"Tête superbement, lourde et violente, front bas, œil prudent, obstiné, chimérique bouche d'orgueil et de terre; étrange vie secrète et cauteleuse, mais tout de même forte et grande, de par un seul dessein poursuivi sans répit de bout en bout, et de par une compréhension singulièrement lucide et précoce de la première condition de la vie intellectuelle parmi les hommes, qui est de les fuir; obscur déclenchement, bref comme un battement d'ailes, du songe dans le poêle d'Allemagne, et de l'appel à philosopher jusqu'à la mort, pour le renouvellement de l'humanité: il nous servirait peu d'étudier la carrière et la physionomie morale de Descartes. C'est son système qui importe; c'est en lui qu'il noue son destin."

The mistake—the 'sin', in fact—of Descartes
was, quite simply, according to M. Maritain, that
he conceived human thought as of the type of
angelic thought: Descartes made thought independent of things—intuitive as to its mode, innate
as to its origins, autonomous as to its nature. But
these, in the Catholic theocracy and in the philosophy of St Thomas Aquinas, are the attributes of
angelic knowledge. The confusion is not merely
theocratic: it is intellectual and logical. It leads,
in the first place, to a denial of the syllogism. The
famous 'method' of Descartes is not properly a
method at all, but merely an impatient rejection
of the essentially discursive nature of human
reasoning. For M. Maritain it is a curious fact
that the first event in the history of rationalism was
a misconception of reason and a renunciation of
the normal conditions of its activity.

The difference between discursive and intuitive
reasoning, which M. Maritain would make a
difference between human and angelic nature, is
only a temporal difference. According to Descartes, our understanding has only one sure mode
of operation: to see. Knowledge is immediate: a
clear and untrammelled vision of the intellect,
apart from and independent of the perceptive
faculties of the body. This knowledge Descartes
calls 'intuitive', and by 'intuition' (*intuitus*) he

means "not the fluctuating testimony of the senses, nor the misleading judgment that proceeds from the blundering constructions of imagination, but the conception which an unclouded and attentive mind gives us so readily and distinctly that we are wholly freed from doubt about that which we understand". And he continues:

"Or what comes to the same thing, intuition is the undoubting conception of an unclouded and attentive mind, and springs from the light of reason alone; it is more certain than deduction itself, in that it is simpler, though deduction cannot by us be erroneously conducted. Thus each individual can mentally have intuition of the fact that he exists, and that he thinks; that the triangle is bounded by three lines only, the sphere by a single superficies, and so on. Facts of such a kind are far more numerous than many people think, disdaining as they do to direct their attention upon such simple matters."

The process of deduction is reduced to the mere manipulation of intuitions; as a process it can discover no truths: it can only present them. From this it follows that knowledge is necessarily an individual experience: it cannot accumulate or be carried on from any given point. Tradition is discredited and learning as such despised. "There is no more need", said Descartes, "for an honest man to know Greek and Latin than Swiss or Low Breton." And this is M. Maritain's great score against Cartesianism: it is the foundation of the characteristic *inhumanity* of modern science. It ignores all that wisdom which is the work of generations; it does not understand the essential rôle of time in the development of human wisdom.

There is another aspect of the Cartesian method equally repugnant to the modern Catholic. The corollary of a mind independent of matter is matter independent of mind. The world becomes a mechanism, and as such only needs to be taken to pieces to be comprehended. And comprehension is easy for the angelic mind. This aspect of Cartesianism is rightly conceived by M. Maritain as the source of that facile rationalism of which we have now reached the absurd limit; it is responsible for the "immense futility of the modern world, and for that strange condition in which we now see humanity—as powerful over matter, as apt and cunning to dominate the physical world, as it is helpless and dismayed before those intellectual realities to which formerly it was linked by the humility of a wisdom subordinate to existence. To struggle against the body it is equipped like a god; but against the spiritual world it has lost all its weapons, and the pitiless laws of the metaphysical world crush it derisively".

The mind no longer measured by things becomes irresponsible: reason has no criterion.
"Under pretext", wrote Bossuet in a letter from
which M. Maritain quotes, "that you can only
admit what you understand clearly—which within
certain limits is very true—anyone is at liberty to
say: I understand this, but I do not understand
that; and on this basis you can approve or reject
whatever you like." This freedom of the mind
from external measures results in every kind of
liberty: in the liberty to be carried away by any
plausible wind of doctrine: "La raison désarmée
perd sa prise sur le réel, et après un temps de
présomption elle est réduite à abdiquer, tombant
alors dans le mal contraire, anti-intellectualisme,
volontarisme, pragmatisme, &c."

The separation of the mind from the material
world was in effect the divorce of science and
philosophy; and it is from this point of view that
Professor Whitehead, in his *Science and the Modern
World*, has brought to a head the scientific reaction against Descartes. This is not a fashionable
nor an emotional change: Descartes still remains of
significance, even for the general reader, as I
shall attempt to show presently. And even for the
scientist his genius still remains "worthy of the
century in which he writes, and of the clearness
of the French intellect. Descartes in his distinction

between time and duration, and in his way of grounding time upon motion, and in his close relation between matter and extension, anticipates, as far as it is possible at his epoch, modern notions suggested by the doctrine of relativity, or by some aspects of Bergson's doctrine of the generation of things".

Then follows the charge made by this modern scientist against Cartesianism: it will be seen not to differ widely in its expression from the charge of M. Maritain:

"But the fundamental principles are so set out as to presuppose independently existing substances with simple location in a community of temporal durations, and, in the case of bodies, with simple location in the community of spatial extensions. Those principles lead straight to the materialistic, mechanistic nature, surveyed by cogitating minds. After the close of the seventeenth century, science took charge of the materialistic nature, and philosophy took charge of the cogitating minds."

It is perhaps easy to find in certain general ideas the determining forces in the history of mankind. It is easier still to ignore such abstract entities. In any case, the development of Cartesianism is clear enough. It begins with the pious aim of demonstrating the certain existence of God; it ends by denying all spiritual values whatsoever. "The independence ascribed to bodily substances carried them away from the realm of values altogether. They degenerated into a mechanism entirely valueless, except as suggestive of an external ingenuity. The heavens had lost the glory of God." Professor Whitehead goes on to show that the doctrine of minds as independent of substances leads directly, not only to private worlds of experience, but also to private worlds of morals. It involves the break-up of all values that cannot be proved within the strictly private world of psychological experience—and that involves, not only all ethical values, but also all æsthetic values (for there is no beauty without an objective and material form). This basic dualism in Cartesianism has often, of course, been contested on metaphysical grounds. But it is only within recent years that science itself has come to realize the insufficiency of a mind independent of objects, and of a theory of objects independent of mind. Professor Whitehead, more definitely than anyone else, has demonstrated the fundamental unity of relationship which exists between mind and matter, and has attempted to embrace within one world-picture the elements of experimental and intuitive knowledge.

In a recent essay M. André Suarès remarked that nothing was lacking in Descartes except poetry; and he probably meant the judgment to be purely descriptive. It is, however, capable of extension, for Descartes' method or system of reasoning is non-poetic in a very profound sense. We have already seen that his first principle of dualism leads to a denial of æsthetic values. Beauty can only be a mechanical harmony, devoid of spiritual animation, deficient in the sense of glory. Such a concept of beauty has, in fact, satisfied certain schools of æsthetic theory. But it has not satisfied the poet himself, who realizes that the forms of his art are part of some larger reality, of some glory beyond the activity of the senses. This universality is precisely what the Cartesian philosophy could not attain, and precisely for that reason no great art has prevailed during the domination of the Cartesian spirit. "La grande vanité de ceux qui n'imaginent pas", wrote Vauvenargues in this connection, "est de se croire seuls judicieux." The real concomitant of Cartesianism is Puritanism, as Professor Whitehead suggests. M. Espinas reached similar conclusions, drawing a parallel between the ideas of Descartes and the paintings of Poussin, the drama of Corneille, and the architecture of the age of Richelieu. All knowledge becomes an invention, an experimental discovery, and all invention a structure of some kind. Poussin's landscapes are 'fabrications', vast assemblages of stage machinery; Corneille's plays are symmetrical arrangements of artificial elements, and even the most moving scenes in his tragedies are draped on the obvious framework of a system.

But to make explicit the non-poetic nature of Descartes' philosophy we must scrutinize a little more closely his use of the term 'intuition'. We have already quoted Descartes' own definition, and this is so admirably precise and clear that it leaves us in no doubt as to the faculty's mode of operation. It is, for Descartes, the only instrument of understanding: it is the light of reason itself. And for a modern reader nothing is so valuable in Descartes as this concentration on the problem of the mind and its machinery. It may be true, as M. Espinas claims, that the Cartesian concept of intuition owes much more to Platonism than has generally been recognized, and is, in fact, but a development of a theory of memory advanced by St Augustine in his *De Ordine*. It would be possible, thought St Augustine, to replace memorized facts by visual images. The inward eye could order before it all objects that the intelligence could conceive. This idea Descartes seized upon and made the basis of his method. First arrange your images, he said, in a mutual dependence, and then, from this chain of images, select groups which offer a certain unity, and of these make another image, common to the group and in relation to the whole series. Such is the method that was to replace the syllogism; such is Cartesian intuition. This method failed, not from any inherent fallacy, but because it was compelled to operate in a dualistic universe. A mind quite independent of the objects of the senses could only know itself. This Descartes thought sufficient; I think, therefore I am. But it is not sufficient merely to affirm existence. We must prove it in detail and in action. Thought is only valid when, like faith, it can move mountains. We are always under the necessity of finding our place within the world of objective facts; and this is precisely what the Cartesians could never do.

We may now push our scrutiny a little further. The mind, we now realize (and perhaps the medieval philosophers realized it too), has certain fixed states of belief which have little to do with the actual process of the understanding: *fides praecedit intellectum*. Such fixed states may be innate ideas, they may be merely ingrained habits of thought. More likely still, for a modern psychologist, they are unconscious rationalizations of personal experience. Now a theory of intuition which presumes, as does the Cartesian theory, that the understanding may proceed from the perception

74

of images to the perception of concepts embodying these images must obviously be in danger of easily accepting for such concepts the promptings of a state of belief. How, that is to say, on such a theory, are you to distinguish between the inspirations of faith and the perceptions of the intuitive faculty?

It is doubtful if they ever were distinguished, and it is possible that we need a new definition and a further limitation of the meaning of the word 'intuition'. This can be secured by limiting the sense of the process to objective apprehension, and this, in its turn, means identifying intuition with the poetic process. For poetry is the apprehension or verbalization of an objective world. The poet must even, as Keats was the first to understand, objectify his own emotions before he can make poetic use of them. Perception is of things, not of abstractions, and intuition is a perceptive process —the only process that perceives things in nakedness rather than in a cloak of secondhand words.

But the world is not a concourse of particulars, and it may be doubted whether intuition can stop at particular things. Its range is not only immediate, but also universal. And for a concept of this wider reality we must return to Professor Whitehead. "We have to admit that the body is the organism whose states regulate our cognisance of

the world. The unity of the perceptual field therefore must be a unity of bodily experience. In
being aware of the bodily experience, we must
thereby be aware of aspects of the whole spatio-
temporal world as mirrored within the bodily life."
Further, Professor Whitehead's theory of organic
mechanism asserts that "an individual entity,
whose own life-history is a part within the life-
history of some larger, deeper, more complete
pattern, is liable to have aspects of that larger
pattern reflected in itself as modifications of its
own being".

This new concept of pattern is very suggestive
for a possible theory of intuition. Pattern is an
event evolved in time. It is spatially 'now', but
only by virtue of its endurance over a definite
lapse of time. To express the same idea inversely,
"endurance is the repetition of the pattern in
successive events". And 'pattern' must in some
way be correlated with 'value'. Value is the outcome of limitation. It is the definition of the
particular pattern. It constitutes the intrinsic
reality of an event. We may visualize an object
with "an unclouded and attentive mind". Such
is perception. We may discover relations between
the visual images thus provided. That is the faculty
of imagination; in poetry it is the invention of
metaphors. There is then a further process and a

higher faculty, and there is at present no better way of describing it than by saying that it is the sudden perception of a pattern in life: the sudden realization of the fact that an organic event, of which we are a part, is in its turn the part of a greater unity, of a unity limited in time and space, formal and harmonious. This further perception or realization is the process to which we might perhaps limit the term 'intuition'; and it is, under the aspect of expression, the process of poetry. In this way poetry involves everything: it is the sense of integral unity without which, not only no poetry, but no philosophy—even no religion—is ever possible.

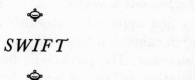

SWIFT

SWIFT

THE prodigious success that awaited *Gulliver's Travels into several Remote Nations of the World* on its first appearance towards the end of the year 1726 came as a great surprise to both author and publisher. The publisher's hasty shifts have been revealed in recent years by various ingenious bibliographers; they have compared page with page, line with line, and word with word, and in the end shown not only that three editions were published within a few weeks but that each of these editions was wholly or partly reset, and that Benjamin Motte, the publisher, unable to meet the demand single-handed, was compelled to utilize the services of more than one printing-house.[1] The first edition, apparently of several thousand copies, seems to have been sold out in about a week. The second edition was published about the middle of November, and the third possibly early in December. Two further editions were published by Motte in 1727, and still another in 1731; and in addition to these there had been two Irish editions and a serial publication in *Parker's Penny Post*. But it is of no account to pursue this

[1] A full account of all that concerns the Motte editions of *Gulliver's Travels* has been given by Mr Harold Williams in the *Library* for December, 1925.

enumeration; what matters is the revelation of the immediateness and completeness of the popularity of this extraordinary book.

Swift himself was not the man to lose his head over such good fortune; fourteen months after the event, in a letter to his publisher, he remarks in his detached way that "the world glutted itself with that book at first, but now it will go off but soberly; but I suppose will not be soon worn out". Not so soon, nor so soberly, as is suggested. *Gulliver* has sold year in year out; it stands with the Authorized Version and *The Pilgrim's Progress* as one of the three great precipitants of modern English usage, and rivals *Robinson Crusoe* in the amplitude of its secular appeal. It will perhaps be profitable to enquire into the causes which underlie this popularity—and this literary appeal; for the first step in any analysis is to realize a distinction here. There have always been two classes: those who are like the old gentleman who went to his map to search for Lilliput (or, more subtly, the bishop who hardly believed a word of it) and those who are like Pope and Arbuthnot and from the first see what the author is driving at. We shall not be far wrong if we ascribe the popularity of the book to the first class, and its position in English literature to the second. For of the first class are all children—of all sizes, ages and epochs—who are open to be beguiled, innocently or ignorantly, by a tale of adventures. It is such as these, whose numbers are legion, that have kept the printing presses busy with these *Travels*: no other proposition is tolerable. For once to look into the dark pain and dreadful bitterness which lie beneath the verisimilitude of *Gulliver* is to resign the cloak of innocence and the mask of ignorance. Those who have found themselves so naked as this in the world are, for good or ill, too few to ensure the popularity of a book.

The critic, of course, must plunge into this harsher element, though he need not stay there: he will find a critical problem in the very popularity of Gulliver. We want to know what the elements are that in this book appeal so infallibly to some instinct within us. It is obvious, of course, that we like to be beguiled—to be taken out of ourselves, to forget ourselves in another world of fancy. It is a mental play-time, the day-dream of our senses, and there is physical ease and rest in the process. But what in *Gulliver* secures this effect? That is the first question to ask, and it is decidedly to the point in any literary enquiry. For it will be found that effects of this kind are purely effects of style. In *Gulliver* we shall find two such distinctive features: the expression is direct and unobstructed, and the development of the narrative is continuous. As for the first of these, Johnson went to the heart of the subject, as he so often did in anything that concerned the technique of writing, when he wrote:

"His style was well suited to his thoughts, which are never subtilised by nice disquisitions, decorated by sparkling conceits, elevated by ambitious sentences, or variegated by far-sought learning. He pays no court to the passions; he excites neither surprise nor admiration; he always understands himself: and his reader always understands him: the peruser of Swift wants little previous knowledge: it will be sufficient that he is acquainted with common words and common things; he is neither required to mount elevations, nor to explore profundities; his passage is always on a level, along solid ground, without asperities, without obstruction."

This is the perfect definition of a popular style, whose essence, apart from the unqualifiable merit of grammatical righteousness, lies in that simplicity which Johnson elsewhere characterized in the remark, "the rogue never hazards a metaphor". The appeal that is latent in all poetry and eloquence is an appeal to a higher and a rarer sensibility; and it was just this appeal which Swift could afford to neglect. He could venture in this

way because he was supported by that other feature
of his style—the economy and coherence of the
narrated action. Of this Johnson's famous remark
was, "when once you have thought of big men
and little men, it is very easy to do all the rest".
But that is a spiteful sally, unworthy of its author.
The actual performance is more wonderful, and
amounts to an extraordinary logic in which, once
a few premises are granted, a whole fabric of history is created, seemingly accurate in its verisimilitude and action. Logic here becomes a substitute
for imagination. In imagination the writer moves
from a foundation of experience to a fictive evoca-
tion whose touchstone is the original experience:
the process is logical in a way. But in *Gulliver*
Swift's whole erection is based on fictive elements;
and the verisimilitude is not due to his selection
of the various elements, but to the way in which
many particulars are deduced from a few general
premises. The make-believe is not one of fancy,
but of effect: we are gulled by the implacable
machinery of the narration, and our interest is not
at all an interest of passion or surprise (to use
Johnson's words), but rather of curiosity and
constructiveness.

In such a manner we can explain the popularity
of *Gulliver*; for these elements—of simplicity, of
make-believe, of 'constructive' rather than of

'creative' elaboration—are the elements which appeal to any mind irrespective of its sensibility or, in a certain sense, its intelligence. But *Gulliver*, of course, does not owe its singular position in the history of English literature to any such adventitious causes: they were quite beside the author's intention in writing the book, and have nothing to do with its implications. Of Swift's purpose we are assured in unequivocal terms that it is solely to vex the world. "Drown the world! I am not content with despising it, but I would anger it, if I could with safety." In these words he exposed his spleen to Pope towards the end of 1725, just about the time he was "finishing, correcting, amending, and transcribing" his *Travels*. And it was in this splenetic mood that the book was born, though it is possible that it was conceived in a happier state. The first hint of the project goes back to 1714, the year of the Scriblerus Club; and there is now no doubt that the actual writing was begun by the spring of 1721.[1] The date is significant; for it was at this time that the drama of his relations with Stella and Vanessa was drawing him into a condition of insupportable anguish, and the state endured until it reached its climax in the death of Vanessa, which was in 1723. We may

[1] See Mr Harold Williams' Introduction to the text of the first edition published by the First Edition Club, 1926.

well believe that the circumstances of her death left Swift in mental anguish greater than any caused by the dilemma of her love for him during her life. But the tremendous distraction of Wood's Halfpence and *The Drapier's Letters* came mercifully at this juncture and occupied his mind the greater part of the succeeding year. But, this incident over, Swift evidently turned once more to the *Travels*,[1] to prolong them and deepen them into that darkness of despair which is their final quality.

It is to the precise definition of this quality that we must now turn. It has commonly been described as irony; and Swift himself gave countenance to the term:

> "Arbuthnot is no more my friend
> Who dares to irony pretend
> Which I was born to introduce,
> Refin'd it first, and shew'd its use."

And Mr Charles Whibley, in his essay on Swift (the Leslie Stephen Lecture for 1917), which is perhaps the most understanding of modern interpretations of the man, strongly underlines this quality, describing Swift as "a great master of irony—the greatest that has ever been born in

[1] Between April and October, 1725, Swift retired from Dublin to a country retreat at Quilca, and there he made his final draft of the *Travels*.

86

these isles. Great enough to teach a lesson to Voltaire himself, and to inspire the author of *Jonathan Wild*".

There exist in the English language a group of terms which, though precise enough when pondered sufficiently, describe subtle variations of temper, and are therefore frequently confused in writing. These are satire, sarcasm, irony, cynicism and the sardonic. It is not suggested that it is possible to define Swift's quality by any one of these terms: it would be possible to find in his writings specimens of them all. But if we consider *Gulliver*, and *Gulliver* is the most significant of all his works, we find in it an obvious consistency of mood which must be designated by a single term. Mr Whibley (like Swift himself) would say irony. But there has been a general tendency to reject this term as too smooth, too suave in its connotation, to fit the savagery of *Gulliver*. Accordingly, the common voice has taken up cynicism. But one of the most convincing passages in Mr Whibley's essay is devoted to a refusal of this term and to a refutation of the charge implied in it:

"Now the cynic may be defined as one who looks upon life and morals with an indifferent curiosity, whose levity persuades him to smile upon the views of others, and to let them go to destruction each his own way. Of this kind of cynicism Swift was wholly innocent. He may be absolved also of that cynicism which the dictionary defines as 'captious fault-finding'. The heart that was torn by *saeva indignatio*, to use a phrase from the epitaph he composed for himself, was no cynic's heart. The truth is that he was a born idealist, with no desire either to snarl or to smile at life. The master-passion of his mind was anger against injustice and oppression."

This is valid criticism, and the only comment necessary is in the nature of a limitation of the word 'idealist'. For there are idealists of fancy and idealists of fact; idealists who would make the world consonant with their abstractions, and idealists who begin with a knowledge of cause and effect, and whose vision is a progressive sense of the issue of trial and error. These latter are better called rationalists; and reason was a very real term with Swift. The grand maxim of his beloved Houyhnhnms was "to cultivate reason, and to be wholly governed by it". The whole basis of the positive part of *Gulliver*, as implied, for example, in the criticisms of the King of Brobdingnag, is rational in the extreme. But this rational idealism was, from a cause which we shall proceed to investigate, brought to nothing by the prevalent pessimism of its author's mind.

Of satire and sarcasm there is, of an incidental

kind, more than enough in *Gulliver*. These elements, we may again conjecture, go back to the early days of the conception; they come earliest in the book, and Arbuthnot and Pope were right in considering them the weakest part of it. The College of Projectors is the most obvious case in point. But if we reject satire and sarcasm as of no real account, and have disposed of cynicism, must we after all fall back on irony, or is there hope in the final term of our list—the sardonic?

All these terms have been clearly defined in Mr Fowler's *Dictionary of Modern English Usage*. The definitions are there arranged in a tabular form, giving separately the motive or aim, the province, the method or means, and the audience, which each word should connote. Of satire the motive is given as 'amendment', the province as 'morals and manners', the method as 'accentuation', and the audience as 'the self-satisfied'. Similarly, sarcasm has for aim 'inflicting pain', for province 'faults and foibles', for method 'inversion', and for audience 'victim and bystander'. These definitions are obvious in their rightness, and the definition of cynicism only shows how justly Mr Whibley has dismissed it from the province of Swift's writings. Its motive is 'self-justification', its province 'morals', its method 'exposure of nakedness', and its audience 'the respectable'. The motive is sufficient to exempt Swift here, however near the method be to that of *Gulliver*. The definition of irony is even more decisive, but, on the other hand, it is perhaps the least adequate of any in Mr Fowler's table. The motive is given as 'exclusiveness', the province as 'statement of facts', the method as 'mystification', and the audience as 'an inner circle'. It is the motive again that defeats any application to Swift; but in this case the audience too is inadequate—or, if not inadequate, too ample. There was, indeed, an inner circle, but it was contracted nearly to a point.

We look finally at the definition of the sardonic. It has for motive 'self-relief', for province 'adversity'; its method is 'pessimism', and its audience 'self'. There is no evidence that the author of this definition had Swift in mind when he made it; but the conjunction of the two brings with it a sense of illumination, and the use of the word in this connection cannot ever again escape us. *Gulliver* responds in all its particulars when once it is considered as the release of a mind from the strain of an intense emotion. It is, perhaps, only too easy to be sentimental about Swift's curious love affairs. The facts are far from complete, and in the absence of facts, to sentimentalize is the easiest course. But the reality of Vanessa's passion is inescapable; and this passion was insinuated, with Swift's complicity, into the rather base and inhuman tyranny of his love for Stella. It is doubtful if any useful analysis can be made of the complex state of Swift's mind at this juncture; what might, by such means, be reduced to a pettiness in his character might equally well be revealed as a tragedy. Signs are not wanting of both possibilities; but, on either supposition, that mind had as issue from its intolerable strain the sardonic pages of *Gulliver*.

The application of these terms cannot be exclusive, and the more precise we make them the less generally can they serve us. But if it be admitted that the special quality of *Gulliver* is sardonic, and that this quality arises out of the special stress of mind under which the work was composed, then it is still possible that the term 'irony' might be of use in the description of a more normal condition of the same mind. The sardonic, that is to say, might presuppose the ironic. This is only true, however, if we abandon the special definition of irony which has been quoted; and this is legitimate because that definition has a special application to literature, being, in fact, the definition of a *genre*. But there is a wider connotation of the word which implies the general sentiment of mockery; and from this sense Swift can hardly be exempted. It would not generally be considered necessary so to exempt him; irony is a fashionable mode, and has to-day an esteem such as it also had in the eighteenth century. It is in this sense the hall-mark of an insincere age; and though Swift is the last man to be accused of a lack of sincerity, yet this provocative display of indirectness is the counterpart of a certain defect of character. This we may illustrate by reference to another age, when a sensitive nature might more honestly express its consciousness of this defect. The following extract is from Renan's intimate account of the life of his sister Henriette—a work surcharged with a kind of beauty totally foreign to the previous century:

"Sa religion du vrai ne souffrait pas la moindre note discordante. Un trait qui la blessa dans mes écrits fut un sentiment d'ironie qui m'obsédait et que je mêlais aux meilleures choses. Je n'avais jamais souffert, et je trouvais dans le sourire discret, provoqué par la faiblesse ou la vanité de l'homme, une certaine philosophie. Cette habitude la blessait, et je la lui sacrifiai peu à peu. Maintenant je reconnais combien elle avait raison. Les bons doivent être simplement bons; toute pointe de moquerie implique un reste de vanité et de défi personnel qu'on finit par trouver de mauvais goût."

Any ironic attitude implies a sense of superiority, which is perhaps the same thing as the 'exclusiveness' of Mr Fowler's definition. And though a sense of superiority may be well grounded in fact, it seldom takes the form of 'ironic philosophy' without involving the possessor of it in a certain vulgarity of sentiment hardly consistent with the right kind of superiority. Renan achieved the right kind precisely for the reason for which his detractors despise him. He came to recognize, as he so frankly states in this passage which we have quoted, that the good is *simply* good, and is not enhanced by oblique or indirect expression. Perhaps in his intimate moods even Swift recognized something of this—the *Journal to Stella* is the best evidence of certain moments of simple goodness; but his general lack of equanimity and directness is bound up with a certain weakness in his character which he was continually betraying. This is the unmeasured vanity of his ambitions and the insistent rancour of his disappointment:

"My greatest misery", he wrote to Bolingbroke in 1729, "is recollecting the scene of twenty years past, and then all of a sudden dropping into the present. I remember, when I was a little boy, I felt a great fish at the end of my line which I drew up almost on the ground, but it dropped in, and the disappointment vexes me to this very day, and I believe it was the type of all my future disappointments."

We might have sympathized more fully if the fish had been a less appropriate metaphor; but it is the type of the very worldly success which Swift always had in mind. Wealth was the immediate object of his desire, and if he could not obtain it by direct means he would have its equivalent in another way:

"All my endeavours from a boy, to distinguish myself, were only for want of a great title and fortune, that I might be used like a Lord by those who have an opinion of my parts—whether right or wrong, it is no great matter, and so the reputation of wit or great learning does the office of a blue ribbon, or a coach and six horses."

This is from a letter to Pope, and there is no reason to doubt the essential truth of the confession, nor its shamelessness. But even this prostitution of his talents might in a sense be condoned if we could be sure that success would have brought him the happiness he longed for; but the innate parsimony of his character forbids that assumption.

There is no evidence to show that Swift entered the Church with any other purpose than the calculating purpose of a careerist. Once committed to that way of life, he seems to have decided

94

that what he could not gain by the talents appropriate to his calling (which he did not possess) he might gain by political intrigue. But at the height of his influence—and no man ever went higher—he found himself waiting in vain for his reward and a bishopric. The dilatoriness of his patrons need not, perhaps, be ascribed to the highest motives—it may be that Swift had made himself too useful a tool to be dispensed with, or too dangerous a one to be released. But it is also conceivable that Harley and Bolingbroke had more judgment than they were credited with, and more respect for the Church; and that they hesitated to confer the dignity of a see on one whose character they knew too well. They, or other advisers of the Queen, may have considered that the author of the *Tale of a Tub*, though endowed with wit, was lacking in learning. And this is the plain truth, if by learning we mean the appropriate mind.

Swift could write quizzically of Dr George Berkeley, as he did in an otherwise kindly letter of recommendation to Lord Carteret; but if he had had more of Berkeley's humility he might have had some of his success. Berkeley is one of the contrasts that best illuminate Swift; for Berkeley had qualities of imagination and speculative intelligence which were totally-wanting in the genius of Swift. Cousin Swift was no poet, as Dryden was the first to see; and, whether we consider him as a writer or as a prospective Bishop, this is a drastic limitation. It is not that it implies a lack of intellectual energy (Swift was inventive enough), but it does qualify the nature of that energy, making it operative on a lower plane and with a narrower range. The poet, who in this sense is not confined to verse, sees beyond his "separate fantasy"; he perceives the "clear universe of things around", and from this perception he derives a sense of sublimity and an eloquence to which Swift was a total stranger.

There is a very significant passage, in one of the letters to Pope which has already been quoted, in which Swift owns a Rochefoucauld as his 'favourite' —"because I found my whole character in him". This is not the only reference to a Rochefoucauld in Swift's correspondence; and from another passage it would seem that he had made Vanessa read his favourite. This direct connection is worth emphasizing; for, though Swift pretended to base his view of human nature on his own observations, it is possible that his mortification was soothed by no other influence so agreeable as the disconsolate philosophy of the French maxim-writer—a philosophy which, like Swift's, was derived from the limited field of Court intrigues and politics rather

han from the world at large. Now a Rochefoucauld has his perfect foil and critic in Vauvenargues; and what Vauvenargues wrote of a Roche-
oucauld very perfectly fits the case of Swift:

"Le duc de La Rochefoucauld a saisi admirable-
ment le côté faible de l'esprit humain; peut-être
n'en a-t-il pas ignoré la force; peut-être n'a-t-il
contesté le mérite de tant d'actions éblouissantes,
que pour démasquer la fausse sagesse. Quelles
qu'aient été ses intentions, l'effet m'en paraît per-
nicieux; son livre, rempli d'invectives contre
'hypocrisie, détourne, encore aujourd'hui, les
nommes de la vertu, en leur persuadant qu'il n'y
en a point de véritable."

This is merely an introduction to a note in
which Vauvenargues does full justice to the real
greatness of a Rochefoucauld. He does, however,
add a qualification relating to the latter's style: a
Rochefoucauld "n'était pas peintre, talent sans
lequel il est bien difficile d'être éloquent"—and
with Vauvenargues, as we shall see in the next
essay, eloquence is the sign of true greatness
(*grandeur d'âme*). It is to Vauvenargues' very
character, indeed, that we should go for a further
contrast; for Vauvenargues in his unhappy life
suffered disappointments quite comparable with
Swift's, but from his state there issued one of the
most equable and courageous views of life that

has ever found expression. Vauvenargues tried to show that the *grandeur d'âme* which was for him the greatest of realities was something as natural as bodily health: it was the power to be superior to one's misfortune and the power to control other men by virtue of one's patience, deeds, or counsels. The error of Swift's philosophy lies in the uniformity and perfection of its pessimism; and the best answer to the misanthropy of *Gulliver* is to be found in these lines of Vauvenargues:

"Les inégalités de la vertu, les faiblesses qui l'accompagnent, les vices qui flétrissent les plus belles vies, ces défauts inséparables de notre nature, mêlée si manifestement de grandeur et de petitesse, n'en détruisent pas les perfections. Ceux qui veulent que les hommes soient tout bons ou tout méchants, absolument grands ou petits, ne connaissent pas la nature. Tout est mélangé dans les hommes; tout y est limité; et le vice même y a ses bornes."

Style is the touchstone of all these matters; and though Swift's style cannot be sufficiently praised for its vigour, clarity and economy, yet it must be recognized that here too Swift has the limitations that belong to his character. Johnson was again percipient in a matter of technique. "For purposes merely didactic" this style is the best of all. "But against that inattention by which known truths are suffered to lie neglected it makes no provision; it instructs, but it does not persuade." Vauvenargues would say it lacks eloquence—not that eloquence of words, which is better called invective, and in which Swift excelled, but the eloquence of ideas and sentiments. In this sense "l'éloquence vaut mieux que le savoir".

"Tout ce qu'on a jamais dit du prix de l'éloquence n'en est qu'une faible expression. Elle donne la vie à tout: dans les sciences, dans les affaires, dans la conversation, dans la composition, dans la recherche même des plaisirs, rien ne peut réussir sans elle. Elle se joue des passions des hommes, les émeut, les calme, les pousse, et les détermine à son gré: tout cède à son voix; elle seule enfin est capable de se célébrer dignement."

Eloquence in this sense is mind's highest reach and widest conquest. It is the creative energy of life itself, manifested on those frontiers which we call variously religion, philosophy and poetry. But in all these forms eloquence was denied to Swift; and without eloquence he was at the mercy of his passions. For a time he could temporize, and so give us *Gulliver's Travels*; but the disruptive forces could not for ever be held in check; and then, as Thackeray said, "thinking of him is like thinking of an empire falling".

$\diamondsuit$

VAUVENARGUES

$\diamondsuit$

VAUVENARGUES

"Revenons avec Vauvenargues à la pureté de la langue, à la sérénité des pensées et à l'intégrité morale"—these words, with which Sainte-Beuve opened his essay on Vauvenargues, announce the three essential aspects of one of the most interesting figures in the history of French literature. Sainte-Beuve saw in Vauvenargues a return, after a period of frivolity and insincerity, to the seriousness of the seventeenth century; he found in his work a presentiment of the new seriousness that was to distinguish the remainder of the eighteenth century. Vauvenargues was born in 1715 and died in 1747; in 1715 Fénelon had died; Bayle had died nine years earlier; Bossuet died in 1704, and Pascal, who was of the same generation, preceded Bossuet by more than forty years. The world in 1715 seemed as empty as it did in 1915, and continued to be empty during Vauvenargues' life as it continues in ours—empty of grace, of faith, of fervour and magnanimity. It is because Vauvenargues revolted against the shallowness of his age that he has a peculiar value for ours, not only because that shallowness has something in common with ours, but more particularly because the experiences of Vauvenargues, and the events which brought about his disillusion and caused his fervour, were very similar to the common experiences and universal events of our own time. His actuality arises from the fact that on the basis of his experiences and out of the depth of his disillusionment he built up a possible philosophy of life.

There is a certain obvious parallelism between the historical situation as it existed at the end of the seventeenth century and beginning of the eighteenth century and the situation that has faced us at the end of the nineteenth century and beginning of the twentieth. A century of genius is behind us as it was behind the contemporaries of Vauvenargues. Genius cannot be manufactured at will, but its works may be made the basis of a tradition. Instead of a tradition, however, the reaction to a period of self-confidence usually takes the shape of a resignation to despair; and just as Vauvenargues' contemporaries turned for their mortification to a typical prophet of despair like La Rochefoucauld, so nowadays, lacking a La Rochefoucauld, we exalt a company of minor prophets. The *Maximes* had the inestimable advantage of precision: to-day our introspective energies must be expended on drearier wastes of self-analysis.

Vauvenargues was the eldest son of an impoverished aristocrat of Aix in Provence. He was destined for the Army because the Army was the only career that a man of his birth and his poverty could honourably embrace. We gather from his letters and from many observations in his writings which bear on his own character that he was by temperament and physique ill-suited to the conditions of army life. This does not mean that he despised the profession of arms or deplored the necessity of wars: he rather tended to idealize military virtues and to see in heroic deeds the only sanction of glory. "Il n'y a pas de gloire achevée sans celle des armes" is one of his own maxims. He saw immediate active service in the War of the Polish Succession, which broke out between France and Italy in 1733. But it was one of the most uninspiring campaigns in history; and though we have no personal records for this period, we can be sure that it offered Vauvenargues few opportunities of testing his idealism. His regiment spent two years in Italy, with little fighting and long intervals of demoralizing idleness. The campaign was a farce, but it took the five years of peace that followed it to complete the disillusionment of a spirit strong enough to survive the disappointments of an inglorious war. For this period we have the evidence of a number of letters written by Vauvenargues to his friends at Aix, the Marquis de Mirabeau and Jules François Paul Fauris de Saint-Vincens. We gather that he had little in common with his fellow-officers, and hated the distractions with which they whiled away their time. Vauvenargues was gentle by nature, plain looking, weak-sighted, and, though not spiritless, timid in physique. He laid himself out to be popular, but he was too diffident to secure that social prestige upon which peace-time promotion depends. Perhaps he took life too seriously: we may be sure that he aroused distrust and suspicion in his companions by his occasional solemnity, his self-consciousness and by all the little awkwardnesses inseparable from a sensitive and reflective habit of mind. The result of the conflict between such a mind and its environment is invariable: the mind retires on itself, idealizes itself and formulates those introverted fantasies which are the material of an imaginative life.

The campaign in Italy had been a farce, but Vauvenargues was not destined to escape the grimmer realities of war. The Bohemian campaign of 1741–3 was one of the most distressful in European history; with the exception of intensive shelling, poison gas and stagnant trenches, it is doubtful if modern war could excel its horrors. Vauvenargues left France with his regiment in July, 1741, as part of an army under the command of the Maréchal de Belle-Isle. In November the French troops assaulted and captured Prague with an ease that proved fatal. For, once ensconced there, they found themselves deserted by their allies the Prussians and surrounded by the hostile Austrians. They were trapped in the city they had so easily captured. The winter went by, and then month by month the following year, with no sign of relief. Supplies became very scarce. By August the French were killing their horses for food, and suffering terribly from want of salt. Rumours of relief, as ever, proved false, and as another winter approached the Army began to despair. Belle-Isle grew desperate, and on the night of December 16 secretly left Prague with fourteen thousand men, and by forced marches hastened across country towards Bavaria. It was the Retreat from Moscow on a smaller scale, but the quality of the misery was the same. Hundreds of men died on the wayside, overcome by fatigue and the intense cold. When the Army after ten days reached friendly territory at Eger, it is related that many of the men collapsed and died, some of them "through having gone too close to the fire". Belle-Isle's forces did not finally reach France until the spring of 1743. There they remained at rest until June, when once again they crossed the Rhine and took part in the battle of Dettingen.

But Vauvenargues was now a broken man. He was permanently injured by frost-bite and had

contracted a lung disease of which he was to die
four years later. He was weary in spirit too. At
Prague he had lost a young friend, Hippolyte de
Seytres, in whose ardour and intelligence Vauvenargues saw the very qualities he had idealized
made actual. Here again Vauvenargues seems to
anticipate one of the bitterest of our recent experiences: we read of Hippolyte de Seytres and
think of Wilfred Owen, of Otto Braun, of Charles
Péguy, and of many others, their names not recorded in elegies. Vauvenargues' *Discours sur les
Plaisirs*, *Discours sur la Gloire*, and *Conseils à un
Jeune Homme*, were all written for De Seytres; and
the fervour of their idealization gives us a measure
of the pathos which lies hidden under the rather
formal periods of the actual 'Éloge funèbre',
which Vauvenargues wrote on his friend. Vauvenargues now began to seek a different path to
glory. On his return from Bohemia he had applied for an appointment at Court, or in the
Diplomatic Service, but without receiving any
acknowledgment. After Dettingen he renewed
his application, none too tactfully. He waited in
vain for a reply, growing more impatient every
day. Finally, in January, 1744, he resigned his
commission, and completely spoilt any chances he
had of other employment by the tone of righteous
indignation with which he invested this action.

He had no money—not even enough to take him to Paris. He negotiated a loan and reached the capital in February. He was not entirely without hope, for during this post-war period he had formed a connection with the most famous writer of the day. This new friend was no less a person than Voltaire, and there is nothing prettier in the history of literature than the way in which the elder man from the first gave understanding and encouragement to this strange aspirant to literary fame. In 1743 Voltaire was already famous throughout Europe. He received from an unknown officer in the Army an essay on the respective merits of Racine and Corneille. Not a very original theme, and not one which was likely to kindle the weary eye of a busy man of letters. But Voltaire read the essay and was impressed. He made enquiries about the social standing of the young officer who had written to him, and was flattered. Miss Wallas in an interesting study which she has devoted to the life and thought of Vauvenargues,[1] gives a good description of what happened:

"Voltaire was pleased by what he heard and pleased by what he had read in Vauvenargues' letter. He loved admiration and gratitude, he was fond of giving literary advice, and he was genuinely

[1] *Luc de Clapiers, Marquis de Vauvenargues.* By Mary Wallas. Cambridge University Press, 1928.

kind. He had already given help and criticism to
a number of struggling young writers, and the
idea of adding an intelligent Army officer to the
mixed collection of his admirers delighted him.
The comparison between Corneille and Racine,
which reflected the usual eighteenth-century preference for Racine, was not very interesting in
itself; and the essay as a whole was slight and
loosely constructed. But Voltaire discerned, and
the fact does honour to his critical powers, the
traces of a fine intelligence in some of Vauvenargues' general reflections on literary 'taste'. The
remark that 'good taste' is 'a quick and true
feeling for natural beauty', and a passage at the
end of the letter describing the differences in taste
which result from individual differences in intelligence and sensitiveness were a proof that the
writer possessed that veiled and discreet type of
originality which the French call 'finesse', and
which even the eighteenth-century critics were not
afraid to admire. ' . . . Depuis que j'entends rai-
sonner sur le goût', wrote Voltaire, 'je n'ai rien
vu de si fin et de si approfondi que ce que vous
m'avez fait l'honneur de m'écrire.' "

Vauvenargues, in common with the aristocrats
of his time and in spite of his genuine urge to
express himself, had hitherto despised the profession of letters, and earlier in his life had rejected

with scorn the suggestion that he should adopt it.
Even now, encouraged by the serious consideration which Voltaire gave to his apprentice essay,
he only thought of using his literary gifts to make
sure of his diplomatic mission. Voltaire, who was
in favour at this time, no doubt helped his cause
considerably, and Vauvenargues seems to have
been definitely promised some employment. He
went home to Aix to await his call, and while
there met with a last malign stroke of fate. He
caught the smallpox, which left him weaker than
ever—his sight almost gone, his face disfigured.
A diplomatic career was now out of the question.
He was reduced to the last and most despised
instrument of glory—the pen. He felt he had very
little longer to live (actually he only lived two
more years); but this time he resolved to devote
to the perfection of a philosophy of life, observing
his own maxim: That to accomplish anything
worth while, a man must always live as if he were
never going to die.

The conversion of a man of action into a man
of letters is a difficult process. Perhaps Vauvenargues was never essentially a man of action—
only such by necessity. The problem in that case
becomes the merely technical one of the conversion of experience into expression. The problem
is made none the easier if experience has led to

disillusionment. Vauvenargues was disillusioned and sick in body and mind, but he differed from most of his modern counterparts in not being deprived of some kind of faith in life. Integrity and courage are useless without this simple faith. The case of Vauvenargues is all the more interesting because the basis of his faith in life was not religious: it was a kind of stoicism. He would probably have accepted the doctrine of original sin in all its essentials, but he refused to convert that dogma into a fatalistic drama, as Pascal did. Original virtue was just as patent to him as original sin; man was stretched between the polarity of good and evil, and not the gift of grace, but the practice of courage, was necessary for salvation. Nevertheless, Vauvenargues is in many senses a disciple of Pascal; Pascal's thought acted as a continual inspiration to him. "He moves the mind", he wrote of Pascal, "startles it and illuminates it and forces it to feel the power of truth"; and this was a deliberate opinion held in the face of Voltaire's derision.

Miss Wallas, in her criticism of Vauvenargues' thought, makes too much of its incompleteness and confusion. She has perhaps fallen into the common error of imagining that the construction of a system of philosophy is a proof of systematic thought; it is more often an elaborate façade

designed to hide a structure of meaner dimensions.
Sainte-Beuve was nearer the truth when he said
that Vauvenargues in his modest fashion brings
to morals something of the universal and all-
embracing genius of a Leibniz—that what he
lacked was no more than time to develop. In his
maxims and scattered fragments we can recognize
not a wayward and merely inquisitive mind but a
universal vision.

"Vauvenargues a l'âme antique"—that is another of Sainte-Beuve's decisive phrases. Like so
many great men, Vauvenargues had been profoundly influenced by the reading of Plutarch's
Lives, as well as by Seneca and the supposed letters
of Brutus to Cicero. There is an enlightening
passage in one of his letters to his friend Mirabeau:

"I used to weep with joy when I read those
Lives; I could never spend a night without speaking to Alcibiades, to Agesilaus and others; I used
to go into the Forum at Rome to harangue with
the Gracchi, or to defend Cato when he was being
stoned. . . . There fell into my hands about the
same time, I don't know by what chance, a volume
of Seneca; and later, some letters which Brutus
wrote to Cicero at the time he was in Greece,
after Caesar's death. These letters are so full of
dignity, fine feeling, passion and courage, that I
found it quite impossible to read them in cold

blood; I read these three books together, and I was so moved that I could no longer restrain the feelings they aroused in me; I choked, I left my books, I tore out like a man in a rage, and ran as hard as I could several times up and down a fairly long terrace, until at last tiredness put an end to my agitation."

Such is the true mode of initiation into the power of eloquence. It is the true initiation into the reality of glory.

"Nowhere else but in those fortunate centuries", Vauvenargues wrote in the same letter to Mirabeau, "does one so well get the measure of the strength and magnitude of the human heart and spirit; liberty reveals, in the very excess of crime, the real greatness of our soul; there the forces of Nature shine out in the depths of corruption; there you have virtue without limits, pleasures without infamy, intelligence without affectation, dignity without vanity, vice without baseness and without disguise."

Vauvenargues was twenty-five when he wrote this letter; the Bohemian campaign was still in front of him, but his analysis of the Roman virtues shows even at that time a certain realism and a recognition of natural imperfections which experience was to confirm. But neither in history nor in life did Vauvenargues find any justification for despair.

Instead of admitting despair, he sought glory. Glory is now a discredited word, and it will be difficult to re-establish it. It has been spoilt by a too close association with military grandeur; it has been confused with fame and ambition. But true glory is a private and discreet virtue, and is only fully realized in solitariness. It is not Vauvenargues, but Traherne in his *Centuries of Meditations*, who has given us the true definition of glory:

"The noble inclination whereby man thirsteth after riches and dominion is his highest virtue, when rightly guided; and carries him as in a triumphant chariot, to his sovereign happiness. Men are made miserable only by abusing it. Taking a false way to satisfy it, they pursue the wind; nay, labour in the very fire, and after all reap but vanity. Whereas, as God's love, which is the fountain of all, did cost us nothing; so were all other things prepared by it to satisfy our inclinations in the best of manners, freely, without any cost of ours. Seeing therefore that all satisfactions are near at hand, by going further we do but leave them; and wearying ourselves in a long way round about, like a blind man, forsake them. They are immediately near to the very gates of our senses. It becometh the bounty of God to prepare them freely: to make them glorious, and their enjoyment easy. For because His love is free, so are His treasures. He therefore that will despise them because he hath them is marvellously irrational: the way to possess them is to esteem them. And the true way of reigning over them is to break the world all into parts, to examine them asunder. And if we find them so excellent that better could not possibly be made, and so made they could not be more ours, to rejoice in all with pleasure answerable to the merit of their Goodness. We being then Kings over the whole world, when we restore the pieces to their proper places, being perfectly pleased with the whole composure. This shall give you a thorough grounded contentment, far beyond what troublesome wars or conquests can acquire."

Vauvenargues often tries to reach such a definition of glory, but its real nature eludes him; it is for him something indefinable. In its essence it is a thing intangible, like light, and light and glory have always been associated together—Heaven, for example, being a City of Light and Glory. In Vauvenargues' sense, glory is the radiance in which virtues flourish. The love of glory is the sanction of great deeds; all greatness and magnanimity proceed not from calculation but from an instinctive desire for the quality of glory. Glory is distinguished from fortune, because fortune exacts care; you must connive with your fellows and compromise yourself in a thousand ways to make sure of its fickle favours. Glory is gained directly, if one has the genius to deserve it: glory is sudden. If we despise glory, it is because we lack virtue.

For Traherne, on the other hand, glory was the sum of all things tangible and concrete:

"By the very right of your senses you enjoy the World. Is not the beauty of the Hemisphere present to your eye? Doth not the glory of the Sun pay tribute to your sight? Is not the vision of the World an amiable thing? Do not the stars shed influences to perfect the Air? Is that not a marvellous body to breathe in? To visit the lungs, repair the spirits, revive the senses, cool the blood, fill the empty spaces between the Earth and Heavens, and yet give liberty to all objects? Prize these first, and you shall enjoy the residue: Glory, Dominion, Power, Wisdom, Honour, Angels, Souls, Kingdoms, Ages."

For such glories man is insatiable, and insatiableness is good. "It is of the nobility of man's soul that he is insatiable." Perhaps the difference between Traherne and Vauvenargues in this respect is that Vauvenargues, like Malory before him and in common with the whole tradition of chivalry, saw in glory a reflection of the esteem of other men; whereas Traherne, more profoundly,

found glory not in the active pursuit of worship
but in the quiet possession of the objective world.
"The service of things and their excellences are
spiritual, being objects not of the eye but of the
mind; and you are more spiritual by how much
more you esteem them." And further:

"Till your spirit filleth the whole world, and
the stars are your jewels; till you are as familiar
with the ways of God in all Ages as with your walk
and table; till you are intimately acquainted with
that shady nothing out of which the world was
made; till you love men so as to desire their happiness, with a thirst equal to the zeal of your own;
till you delight in God for being good to all: you
never enjoy the world. Till you more feel it than
your private estate, and are more present in the
Hemisphere, considering the glories and the
beauties there, than in your own house: till you
remember how lately you were made, and how
wonderful it was when you came into it: and more
rejoice in the palace of your glory, than if it had
been made but to-day morning."

Traherne's doctrine proceeds from metaphysical
meditation, Vauvenargues' from action; but both
are spiritual. But Vauvenargues' doctrine is more
limited, its sources being in individual experience
rather than in universal knowledge. In so far as
his faith was reinforced by reading, it was such

as Plutarch provided, and in Plutarch glory is the reward only of heroes. Perhaps this was Vauvenargues' fundamental belief. But he had already discerned, in his *Introduction à la Connaissance de l'Esprit humain,* an essential connection between glory and eloquence. There are two kinds of eloquence—the eloquence of words, which consists in saying with ease and aptness whatever comes into one's head; and the eloquence of ideas or sentiments, which force their own appropriate expression. The latter kind is true eloquence, and it is a characteristic of all great men, not merely of great writers. Eloquence is the expression of glory: glory in words, not of words.

Vauvenargues' own experience tended to show that action alone could not encompass glory; that fate and the imperfections of fortune easily overwhelm the strongest will. Any career involving relations with other men is impure to that extent. All virtue is the outcome of a solitary strife. Glory is solitary. All that can be gained openly is the fame that is dependent on fortune. Glory must be sought in the interior court of Traherne's great asseveration: "To think well is to serve God in the interior court." There the act is direct eloquence. Sensation and idea unite to create the exact image of truth. Vauvenargues himself said:

"Those who are born eloquent speak with such

great clearness and brevity on great subjects, that most other people do not realize that they are speaking with profundity. Sophists and cold calculating spirits fail to recognize philosophy when eloquence gives it a universal appeal, daring to paint the truth in bold and vigorous strokes. They treat as superficial and frivolous this splendour of expression which is in itself the hall-mark of great thoughts."

There is, in this and in all Vauvenargues' observations on truth, a feeling for what later in the century came to be known as 'sentiment'. He distrusted the 'reason', both in the seventeenth-century sense of austerity, severity and repression, and in the eighteenth-century sense of scientific materialism. "La raison nous trompe plus souvent que la nature" was one of his maxims. Vauvenargues let some personal quality, which we can only vaguely call 'tenderness', colour his thoughts. "Les grandes pensées viennent du cœur" is one of his most famous sayings, but it is meant in no sentimental fashion. He anticipates Rousseau, but not Rousseau's abasement of the intellect. There is a saving virtue in Vauvenargues' epithet 'grandes'. It implies eloquence, and eloquence, as we have seen, is glory sublimated. Glory is far from any conception we may have of Rousseau. The tenderness of Vauvenargues is no more than a sense of the instinctive basis of so much of our life. Miss Wallas remarks:

"There existed in Vauvenargues' mind a distinction, inherited through centuries from the earliest Greek thinkers, between the 'natural' or instinctive and the acquired or artificial elements in human behaviour. He felt that 'passion' was one of the most unalterable elements in man because it was one of the most 'natural', and that the 'reason' of the Stoics and the Cartesians was something fundamentally artificial, imposed upon man from without."

Miss Wallas, in her final judgment of Vauvenargues, makes this quality at once his advantage and his shortcoming:

"The permanent value, not only of Vauvenargues' psychology of thinking, but of his whole literary work, depends on the degree to which his inborn power of sensitive and vivid observation was brought into play, and the extent to which it was either intensified or blurred by the angry feelings aroused by his experience. His attempt to construct a new ethic was, taken as a whole, a failure, because, whereas sensitive introspection is the most valuable of all qualities to a psychologist, we ask of the moralist who undertakes to judge the permanent value of varied human experience, that he should possess, besides psychological ac-

curacy, singleness of purpose, breadth of understanding, and intellectual consistency. Vauvenargues' ethical purpose was confused by the
tumult of his feelings, and by a half-conscious
desire to justify the actions and motives of his own
life. He could not form a consistent ethic for other
men, because he was incapable of reconciling the
conflict between the emotions of ambition, timidity
and kindness in his own soul."

This is excellent criticism, but is the judgment
quite fair? Nothing is more true, and no truth
more in need of enforcement to-day, than that
the spheres of pure thought and of emotion
should be kept distinct. Our philosophy suffers
from emotional bias, and our religion from a mis-
taken attempt to rationalize it. But Vauvenargues
was concerned with neither religion nor with pure
thought. He saw quite clearly that religion is an
affair of the emotions, and he left it at that. To
pure thought he had no pretensions. Perhaps he
thought of it as a phantom category, for in one of
his maxims he says: "On ne s'élève point aux
grandes vérités sans enthousiasme; le sang-froid
discute et n'invente point; il faut peut-être autant
de feu que de justesse pour faire un véritable
philosophe." Apart from pure thought and religion, what is left? Miss Wallas mentions ethics,
morals, and those calvinistic virtues, singleness of

purpose, breadth of understanding, and intellectual consistency. Every system of ethics that has been inspired by such aims as these lies like a heap of bleached bones in the waste of time. The code of human behaviour is an illusion; there is only the science of individual behaviour, which is psychology; and Vauvenargues is a superb psychologist. So is Pascal. Miss Wallas' strictures apply equally to that other genius in many ways so complementary to Vauvenargues. Pascal and Vauvenargues—between them they embrace all the variations of the human soul, from its deepest subjection in emotion to its highest intellectual glory. Vauvenargues confesses in one place, that if such talents could exist side by side, he would like to think like Pascal, to write like Bossuet, and to talk like Fénelon. Perhaps he did none of these things in the degree of his exemplars, but perhaps he added another talent to these three; so that now we can wish to think like Pascal, to write like Bossuet, to talk like Fénelon, and to live like Vauvenargues.

STERNE

STERNE

"I f they have a fault", Sterne said of the French, "they are too *serious*." The Count in *A Sentimental Journey* received this statement as a pleasantry, but, says the author, "it was my most settled opinion." The Count could not wait for reasons, and this we must regret, for probably Sterne would have enforced the corollary of his statement, namely, that if you would know the wittiest, most whimsical and most humorous nation in the world, seek the English. It is a great pity that Sterne did not make this claim for us, for no one since has had the courage. We have found it more profitable to keep up a pretence of native phlegm and melancholy, and Bagehot, as we shall see in a later essay, described our greatest political asset as stupidity. In literature we admit 'homely humour', but if by any chance we find ourselves blessed with an author remarkable for wit, we search hastily for some foreign strain in his ancestry. We are never happy until we have made him an Irishman, or better still, if he is really wicked, a Frenchman. This has been Sterne's fate. He is very droll, it cannot be denied; the drollest of all our writers. But then he was born in Ireland of a mother who may have been partly French and of a father who was mainly a Yorkshireman.

What, then, was Sterne? Nothing that can be measured. An individual is born as a merely potential quality: both before and after his birth the possible variations in his development are determined by a thousand chances. A work of art, on the other hand, is born to a finite shape. Its growth is completed at birth, and for that reason it is much more to the point to enquire into the birth and parentage of a work of art than into those of its author. The significant fact is that *Tristram Shandy* was written by a Yorkshire parson who had never moved far from his parish for more than twenty years. We might go further and say that it was written by a man whose interests and passions were purely local, and that it was, primarily, written for a local public. Its close relation to its immediate predecessor, the satire on local affairs known as *The History of a Good Warm Watch-Coat*, should be borne in mind. *Tristram Shandy* is an epic of Yorkshire life, and this fact is only an illustration of the profound truth that all the great epics of the world are local epics. From the *Iliad* to *Don Quixote* they were all generated in a small society, and took on their universality by virtue of the genius that enabled each of their authors to see a world in his particular grain of sand. It is almost possible to say that an epic needs for its creation the all-inclusive self-

consciousness of a small community. The ideal
conditions exist when you have a community large
enough to employ all the capacities and exhibit
all the passions of mankind, yet small enough to
be within the knowledge and observation of one
man. Such a community existed in York in the
eighteenth century. It was an autonomous society,
independent of London. As a city it was a centre
of social life, with its own learned societies and
coffee-houses, its theatre and racecourse. Its
ancient history, its ecclesiastical pre-eminence,
and its civic dignities, these endowed it with the
necessary density of tradition. Life was seen
against a background. A prebendary of the
cathedral church, such as Sterne, with a parish
within an easy amble, was at the heart of this
miniature world, and could watch, and take part
in, the variety and intensity of its serio-comic life.
He could compass the whole scale between the
yokels of his own parish at Sutton and the Arch-
bishop in his palace at Bishopthorpe. And within
this compass lies the comic world of *Tristram Shandy*.

Sterne is a popular author—surely more popular
than Fielding or Richardson or Smollett, though
not, alas, so popular as Dickens. But in a critical
sense English authors are neglected in the measure
of their popularity. English critics seem to assume
that because an author is accepted, there is no

need to explain his achievement. So most of the essays which have been written on Sterne are lacking in interest or freshness: they are confined to admirable acquiescence in his sense of humour and fierce denunciation of his impropriety. Thackeray's lecture is positively splenetic in tone, and seems to possess a violence and a baselessness more worthy of psychological than critical attention. Here are some of the epithets hurled at Sterne or his work in the course of a few pages: 'Coward'; 'wretched'; 'worn-out old scamp'; 'vain, wicked, witty, and false'; 'this actor, this quack'; 'an impure presence'; 'foul satyr'; 'poor wretch'; 'horrible baseness of blasphemy'; 'cheap dribble'; and so on. A critic who uses such thoughtless expletives is obviously not going to bother much about the extenuating genuineness of his subject; it is not easy, even for an unprejudiced mind, to balance morality against art. Walter Bagehot made a better attempt: his view is not unprejudiced—whose could be in that circumspect age?—but there is genuine insight in a passage like the following:

"The real excellence of Sterne is single and simple: the defects are numberless and complicated. He excels, perhaps, all other writers in mere simple description of common sensitive human action. He places before you in their simplest form the elemental facts of human life; he does not view them through the intellect, he scarcely views them through the imagination; he does but reflect the unimpaired impression which the facts of life which does not change from age to age make on the deep basis of human feeling, which changes as little though years go on. . . . Sterne's feelings in his higher moments so much overpowered his intellect, and so directed his imagination, that no intrusive thought blemishes, no distorting fancy mars, the perfection of the representation. The disenchanting facts which deface, the low circumstances which debase the simpler feelings oftener than any other feelings, his art excludes. The feeling which would probably be coarse in the reality is refined in the picture. The unconscious tact of the nice artist heightens and chastens reality, but yet it is reality still. His mind was like a pure lake of delicate water: it reflects the ordinary landscape, the rugged hills, the loose pebbles, the knotted and the distorted firs perfectly and as they are, yet with a charm and fascination that they have not in themselves. This is the highest attainment of art, to be at the same time nature and something more than nature."

That is excellent criticism, vividly written and definitely illuminating. But the fuss Bagehot

makes about the indecency of *Tristram Shandy* and
its general unfitness for young ladies would make
modern young ladies open their eyes with wonder.
What the Victorian critics did not realize—could
not realize, because of their lack of frankness in
sexual matters—was the triviality of the question
on which they expended so much energy. Coleridge
alone leads us to the essentials of the theme. There
is more real criticism in his fragmentary notes on
Sterne than in the whole body of anything else
written on the same subject. It is true that at
first sight he would seem to feel as strongly as
Thackeray or Bagehot on the question of Sterne's
licentiousness—but with this difference: he not
merely condemns it, but also analyses it. It is his
analysis of the question that more than ever
reveals its essential triviality. And when Coleridge
says that "Sterne cannot be too severely censured
for using the best dispositions of our nature [he
is thinking of the characters of Mr Shandy, Uncle
Toby, and Trim] as the panders and condiments
for the basest", he thereby suggests the possible
defence that these dispositions gain by their juxta-
position with a shade of evil. Uncle Toby is not
so much a butt to this kind of wit, as the illustration of its insufficiency.

Coleridge in his lecture "on the nature and
constituents of humour" distinguishes humour

from the different kinds of wit. Wit is impersonal, consisting wholly in the understanding and the senses. It is a play with words, or with thoughts, or with images. But "no combination of thoughts, words, or images will of itself constitute humour, unless some peculiarity of individual temperament and character be indicated thereby, as the cause of the same". And Coleridge, to illustrate his meaning, compares the comedies of Congreve with Falstaff, and with Sterne's Corporal Trim, Uncle Toby, and Mr Shandy. That is the first point established by Coleridge's analysis—the dependence of humour upon personality. The second point is equally important. In Coleridge's own words: "there always is in a genuine humour an acknowledgment of the hollowness and farce of the world, and its disproportion to the godlike within us". If we combine these two observations we might say that humour is an exposure of the contrast between the godlike and the trivial exhibited in a personality. But Coleridge probed deeper still, to ask: "Is there some one humorific point common to all that can be called humorous?" He thought there was and that it consisted in "a certain reference to the general and the universal, by which the finite great is brought into identity with the little, or the little with the finite great, so as to make both nothing in comparison with the infinite. The little is made great, and the great little, in order to destroy both; because all is equal in contrast with the infinite. 'It is not without reason, brother Toby, that learned men write dialogues on long noses'". And Coleridge adds: "Humorous writers, therefore, as Sterne in particular, delight, after much preparation, to end in nothing, or in direct contradiction."

Coleridge makes one further and more subtle distinction in the case of Sterne which must be referred to before returning to Sterne himself. He puts as first among the excellences of Sterne his ability "in bringing forward into distinct consciousness those minutiæ of thought and feeling which appear trifles, yet have an importance for the moment, and which almost every man feels in one way or another. Thus is produced the novelty of an individual peculiarity together with the interest of a something that belongs to our common nature. In short, Sterne seizes happily on those points, in which every man is more or less a humorist. And, indeed, to be a little more subtle, the propensity to notice these things does itself constitute the humorist, and the superadded power of so presenting them to men in general gives us the man of humour. Hence the difference of the man of humour, the effect of whose portraits does not depend on the felt presence of himself, as humorist, as in the instances of Cervantes and Shakespeare—nay, of Rabelais too; and of the humorist, the effect of whose works does very much depend on the sense of his own oddity, as in Sterne's case, and perhaps Swift's: though Swift again would require a separate classification".

Coleridge gives us here a very clear indication of the singularity of Sterne's genius. If there is one characteristic which distinguishes Sterne from his fellow-humorists, it is certainly the 'felt presence' of the man in his work: the author himself is the real hero of *Tristram Shandy*. And in this matter Sterne was very much of his age. He was born within a year of the birth of Rousseau, and though it would be difficult to maintain that there was any direct communication of ideas, yet there were common influences at work, and these influences produced similar fruit. There are, of course, many differences: there is nothing of Rousseau's romantic naturalism about Sterne, and he is too much a creature of common sense to discard the rational framework of religion and society. But when all these differences have been discounted there remains a common doctrine of sensibility which is fundamental to both men. It was the same doctrine, but very differently interpreted. In Rousseau the doctrine was applied inwardly, to his own feelings, until his own sensibility be-

came the only value and his own sanctity the pre-
dominating illusion. But in Sterne the doctrine
is applied outwardly: it is sympathetic: it is a
measure, not merely of the intensity of his own
feelings, but of the definite reality of his fellow-
men. Spontaneity is perhaps the only word which
can be applied without qualification to both
Rousseau and Sterne: that quality they had in
common. It only became differentiated when, in
Rousseau's case, it was corrupted by egoism. But
incidentally we may note that this freedom of
sensibility, this spontaneity, had quite parallel
effects in the development of prose style in France
and in England. In this matter Rousseau and
Sterne occupy almost precisely similar positions.
They break down the dignity, the orotundity
and the volubility of their predecessors and
give us instead a prose that is vivid, nervous
and swift.

The nineteenth-century conception of Sterne as
a ribald prelate has quite blinded us to the truth
that he was in reality a writer with a purpose, a
moral preceptor, a subtle intelligence that masked
beneath his humour and licentiousness the kindly
philanthropy of his age—the age of Shaftesbury
and Hutcheson. Coleridge asked his audience to
note "Sterne's assertion of, and faith in, a moral
good in the characters of Trim, Toby, etc., as

contrasted with the cold skepticism of motives
which is the stamp of the Jacobin spirit". And
in an Advertisement to his sermon on the Abuses
of Conscience—Yorick's sermon in *Tristram Shandy*,
but published separately in 1766—Sterne himself
referred to *Tristram Shandy* as "a moral work,
more read than understood". This perfectly
serious claim on his part is borne out by another
equally serious reference to the *Sentimental Journey*
made in a letter of November 12, 1767, addressed to
Mr and Mrs James: "My design in it was to teach
us to love the world and our fellow-creatures better
than we do—so it runs most upon those gentle
passions and affections, which aid so much to it."

This paradox of a moral Sterne will be found
more acceptable when the world begins to read that
neglected half of Sterne's genius—his Sermons.
There is no inconsistency—in style, in manner,
and in sincerity and aim—between the Sermons and
Tristram Shandy or the *Sentimental Journey*. Since
their first success no one seems to have bothered to
read the Sermons; certainly Thackeray had not
seen them, and Bagehot does not seem to have considered them for long. It is unfortunate because
there, more explicitly than in his works of fiction,
Sterne reveals his approach to life. In the opening
passage of his sermon on the Prodigal Son he
makes this very significant statement:

"I know not whether the remark is to our honour or otherwise, that lessons of wisdom have never such a power over us, as when they are wrought into the heart, through the groundwork of a story which engages the passions. Is it that we are like iron, and must first be heated before we can be wrought upon? or, Is the heart so in love with deceit, that where a true report will not reach it, we must cheat it with a fable, in order to come at truth?"

The preacher does not stop to answer his questions: they are rhetorical. But he answered them in his works, which are, as he meant them quite simply to be, stories which engage our passions and by that experience teach us "to love the world and our fellow-creatures better than we do"—such love being, Sterne ever maintained, the beginning and the end of all wisdom.

This metaphor of the iron heated until it can be wrought upon, this stress upon the passions and affections, was not with Sterne the commonplace that it might seem to us. There was, at the back of it, the groundwork of a philosophy, and though it may be freely admitted that no one is on the surface less philosophical than Sterne, yet when we dive below the surface we find that he was everywhere indebted to philosophy, and in particular to the philosophy of John Locke.

In his *Life and Times of Laurence Sterne* Professor Wilbur Cross has drawn attention to an interesting volume of memoirs published in Paris in the year 1820—*Mémoires historiques sur la Vie de M. Suard, sur ses Écrits, et sur le XVIIIe siècle* by Dominique Joseph Garat, where there is to be found a long and extremely interesting account of Sterne, based on the recollections of M. Suard. Suard was later a famous Academician—it was due to his efforts that the Academy survived the Revolution. In his youth he became friendly with Sterne during the latter's stay in Paris, and had read and appreciated *Tristram Shandy*. He had intimate discussions with Sterne on many subjects, and on one occasion asked him what were the influences which had determined the cast of his genius. Sterne's reply is extremely illuminating. There is no question of Suard's embroidery: the self-analysis is too exact, too penetrating, for anyone but Sterne himself to have expressed it. The first source of his originality, he said, was "an organization in which predominated the sacred principle which forms the soul, that immortal flame which nourishes life and yet devours it, which suddenly exalts and modifies all sensations, and which we call *imagination* or *sensibility*, according as it is used to depict scenes or to portray passions; the second source of his originality was the daily reading of the Old and New Testaments, books which were as agreeable to his taste as they were necessary to his profession; and the third source was the study of Locke, which he had begun in his youth and continued through all his life; those who knew the philosopher well enough to recognize his presence and his influence will find them or sense them on every page, in every line, and in the choice of all his expressions; this philosopher, who was too religious to want to explain the miracle of sensation, but who, with this miracle which he does not dare to question but accounts to God, unfolds all the secrets of the understanding, avoids all errors, and arrives at positive truths; a holy philosophy, without which there will never be on earth either a true universal religion or a true system of morals or man's complete power over Nature".[1]

We have in this confession a most important clue to the real understanding of Sterne. Now, of the three explanations which Sterne gives of his genius, the first and the third have a direct connection. The doctrine of sensibility in which Sterne found an explanation of his creative energy, and to which he made his writings subservient—this doctrine arises out of the philosophy of Locke. The main object of Locke was to destroy the

[1] Garat, *op. cit.*, vol. II, pp. 149-50.

scholastic dogma of innate principles and to explain all knowledge as the product of sensation or
reflection. The emphasis was very much on the
sensations, and sensation, with its related word
'sensibility', was very much on men's lips during
the first half of the eighteenth century. It was the
catchword of that age, in the way that 'relativity'
is the catchword of ours.

I must digress at this point into that very interesting pursuit—the history of words. There is
nothing more salutary, both for our self-esteem
and our critical rectitude. The particular group
of words we are concerned with—those originating
out of the word 'sense'—have a most complicated
history, and might very well be made to illustrate
the whole development of philosophy and taste
since the seventeenth century. But for the moment we are concerned only with the word 'sentimental'. It is a word which, though not invented
by Sterne, was nevertheless given universal cur-
rency by him. The date of the first use of the word
recorded by the *Oxford English Dictionary* is 1749.[1]
Lady Bradshaigh writes to Samuel Richardson:

"What in your opinion is the meaning of the
word *sentimental,* so much in vogue among the

[1] I have discussed in an Introduction to the *Sentimental Journey*
published earlier in this year by the Scholartis Press the possibility
that Sterne himself used the word as early as 1740.

polite. . . . Everything clever and agreeable is comprehended in that word. . . . I am frequently astonished to hear such a one is a *sentimental* man; we were a *sentimental* party; I have been taking a *sentimental* walk."

This shows us the word in its first usage. It meant 'characterized by sentiment' and 'sentiment' meant sensation—Locke's sensation—in its personal aspect. But as the word got bandied about among the illiterate, or at any rate among the unphilosophical, it lost the definiteness of its impress and came to signify something at once more limited and less exact. A sentiment was, by the middle of the eighteenth century, any refined or tender emotion, especially those portrayed in literature and art. But the emphasis was on the refinement, as we see from Lady Bradshaigh's letter, and this was the implication of the word as used by Sterne. The *Sentimental Journey* (1768) was one involving and exhibiting delicate feelings. That these delicate feelings sometimes lead us into indelicate situations does not alter the meaning of the word. But the word did alter in meaning, though not in the direction of indelicacy. In 1823 Southey wrote: "Rousseau addressed himself to the sentimental classes, persons of ardent or morbid sensibility, who believe themselves to be composed of finer elements than the gross multitude." The word is already, more than a hundred years ago, beginning to imply something excessive. In 1826 Disraeli speaks of "a soft sentimental whisper"; in 1827 Scott of "a sentimental tear". And so the degeneration of the word proceeds, until in 1862 we have Miss Braddon writing: "You have no sentimental nonsense, no silly infatuation . . . to fear from me." Nowadays it can be used for the extreme stages of emotional deliquescence.

It cannot be doubted that Sterne's reputation has suffered unjustly from this degeneration of the word 'sentimental'. In the modern sense, Sterne is not sentimental; he is almost cynical, which is the opposite quality. But he is not really cynical; he is just humorous. It must be admitted that there are passages in *Tristram Shandy* and *A Sentimental Journey* which border on the modern sense of sentimentality. But they keep beyond the border. Sterne's intelligence is always there, ready to play with, to play on, your "gentler passions and affections"; but he always saves himself, either by a perfect control of expression (that is, by the technique of his style), or, more remarkably, by a sudden humorous recovery—as in his famous encounter with the disconsolate Maria:

"They were the sweetest notes I ever heard; and I instantly let down the fore-glass to hear them more distinctly—'Tis *Maria*, said the postillion, observing I was listening—Poor *Maria*, continued he (leaning his body on one side to let me see her, for he was in a line betwixt us), is sitting upon a bank, playing her vespers upon her pipe, with her little goat beside her.

"The young fellow uttered this with an accent and a look so perfectly in tune to a feeling heart, that I instantly made a vow I would give him a four-and-twenty sous piece when I got to *Moulins*—

"—And who is *poor Maria?* said I.

"The love and piety of all the villages around us, said the postillion—it is but three years ago that the sun did not shine upon so fair, so quick-witted and amiable a maid; and better fate did *Maria* deserve than to have her Banns forbid by the intrigues of the curate of the parish who published them—

"He was going on, when *Maria*, who had made a short pause, put the pipe to her mouth, and began the air again—they were the same notes;—yet were ten times sweeter: It is the evening service to the Virgin, said the young man—but who has taught her to play it, or how she came by her pipe, no one knows; we think that Heaven has assisted her in both, for ever since she has been unsettled in her mind it seems her only consolation—she has never once had the pipe out of her hand, but plays that service upon it almost night and day.

"The postillion delivered this with so much discretion and natural eloquence that I could not help deciphering something in his face above his condition, and should have sifted out his history had not poor *Maria* taken such full possession of me.

"We had got up by this time almost to the bank where *Maria* was sitting: she was in a thin white jacket, with her hair, all but two tresses, drawn up into a silk net, with a few olive leaves twisted a little fantastically on one side—she was beautiful; and if ever I felt the full force of an honest heartache it was the moment I saw her—

"—God help her! poor damsel! above a hundred masses, said the postillion, have been said in the several parish churches and convents around, for her—but without effect. We have still hopes, as she is sensible for short intervals, that the Virgin at last will restore her to herself; but her parents, who know her best, are hopeless upon that score, and think her senses are lost for ever.

"As the postillion spoke this, *Maria* made a cadence so melancholy, so tender and querulous, that I sprang out of the chaise to help her, and found myself sitting betwixt her and her goat before I relapsed from my enthusiasm.

"*Maria* look'd wistfully for some time at me, and then at her goat—and then at me—and then at her goat again, and so on, alternately—

"—Well, *Maria*, said I, softly—What resemblance do you find?"

Here, of course, the goat saves the situation. We come back to Coleridge's definition of humour: "The little is made great, and the great little, in order to destroy both; because all is equal in contrast with the infinite."

If the injustice done to Sterne by our modern degradation of the word 'sentimentality' were generally admitted, then we could more safely use the cognate word 'sensibility' to describe the general background of his work. It has usually been assumed that it had no background. Critics have taken too literally Sterne's joke, that having written one word he trusted to Providence for the next. They have been deceived by their inability to appreciate the method of *Tristram Shandy* into thinking not merely that it had no method (there is some excuse for that fault, for it is a subtle matter), but also into imagining that where there was no method there was no mind. That was because they were incapable of taking this humorist seriously. It may be urged that no one should take a humorist seriously, but apart from the fact that this shows a misconception of humour, why should Sterne be treated any less seriously than his compeers? Rabelais and Cervantes have been treated with perfect seriousness, and learned works have been written, not on their humour, but on their thought. In the case of Rabelais and Cervantes an intellectual quality is obvious enough. To keep to Locke's differentiation, their ideas were derived from reflection; whereas, in Sterne's case, the ideas were derived mainly from sensation. The background in his case was *sensibility*; and sensibility is intimately related to *conscience*; and conscience to *morality*. And between these states of mind—they are but different aspects of the same state of mind—there is involved the element of humour. And one of the most significant things about Sterne is that he makes this interrelation of elements so clear.

His favourite sermon was the one he included in *Tristram Shandy*: that on the Abuses of Conscience. His theme was, that in conscience there is no inherent goodness; it is not a law unto itself, infallible or invariable. Conscience is rather a principle, 'seated within the mind, which enables us to interpret our conduct in the light of laws that are already given us in Religion and Morality. Conscience, in fact, is moral sensibility, but it is a sensibility operating within a fixed world. This is anything but a romantic doctrine; it is, indeed, the essential classical doctrine. And that is why, in spite of his popularity among some of the romantics, Sterne's genius is really to be reckoned on the side of the classical forces in literature.

His humour is evidence of that. All real humorists are classicists, because it is in the nature of a classicist to see things finite, and see things infinite, but not to confuse these two categories. The classicist, like the humorist, acknowledges the "hollowness and farce of the world, and its disproportion to the godlike within us"—and this is Coleridge's definition of humour. It might just as well be a definition of classicism. The romantic, on the other hand, merges all things into the infinite, sees all men as gods, or, at the other extreme, sees nothing but the unrelated trivialities of existence—the jumble, the glitter, the breathless jollity of it all.

We have, then, this inner principle which we may call conscience and which is the sense of religion and of morality; or we may call the same principle sensibility, and then it is the sense of humour. And it is a curious fact, which Coleridge has pointed out, that we find no real humour among the ancients:

"Humour took its rise in the Middle Ages; and the Devil, the Vice of the Mysteries, incorporates the modern humour in its elements. It is a spirit measured by disproportionate finites. The Devil is not, indeed, perfectly humorous; but that is only because he is the extreme of all humour."

That is a very profound observation, and suggests as a possible truth that the greatest degree of humour is the complement of the greatest degree of religion. Old Nick, as he was good-humouredly called, only lost his reality because he became divested of his humour, gradually becoming a figure of horror as his significance and power passed from the realm of the finite and physical to that of the infinite and metaphysical.

There remain two very important aspects of Sterne's genius, which must be briefly touched upon in any general estimate of his place in literature—namely, his mastery of English prose style and his mastery of the art of narrative. His style is one of deceptive ease, but we know that it cost him great pains. The first draft of the first two volumes of *Tristram Shandy* was written rapidly —in less than six months; but an interval of another six months elapsed before the volumes were published, and during this time the manuscript was circulated and met with a good deal of criticism. As a result of these criticisms and of his own reflection, Sterne is said to have reduced the bulk of the volume by half. "I have burnt more wit than I have published" was his own confession. And we know from the evidence of his Letter Book that even in matters of ordinary correspondence he exercised extraordinary care, drafting and

emending and copying out even the most intimately trivial notes.

We have in Suard's memoir, which has been
quoted, the secret of his style—perhaps not the
'secret', because that is an impalpable energy
which defies analysis—but at least its more formal
origins. These are to be found in his confessed
devotion to the literature of the Bible and to the
writings of Locke. Of the Bible he has spoken
elsewhere, in that sermon which Newman praised
in his *Idea of a University*. The distinction which
Sterne makes between true and false eloquence
shows his real understanding of the art of writing,
and his definition of true eloquence as "a surprising mixture of simplicity and majesty" is one
of quite excellent exactness. His indebtedness to
Locke in this matter might not have been sus-
pected but for the solemn declaration of his devotion to this philosopher which he made to
Suard; but on comparing the styles of Locke and
Sterne we find a decided similarity. It is not easy
to eliminate the humour of the one and the
abstract reasoning of the other and pierce to the
radical elements of their composition and rhetoric.
But if we admit the unity of style between Sterne's
Sermons and his humorous works—and anyone
who has read both will not be disposed to deny
this unity—and then compare the two authors on

a cognate or identical subject,[1] the resemblance is found to be very remarkable. But the source of his style does not matter so much as its significance. There can be no doubt that it·has had a decisive effect on the development of English prose style in deflecting it from the path of latinization into which it had entered during the second half of the seventeenth and first half of the eighteenth centuries. Sterne, more than any other writer of his age, re-established the native tradition, returning to the original genius of the language and making the basis of his style an English idiom that had been lost almost since Milton's day.

As examples of his expressive power there is almost every paragraph of *Tristram Shandy* and *A Sentimental Journey*. No books in English literature are so consistently brilliant and vivid in their style. An ease of rhythm and limpidity of phrase continue page after page and never dissipate into the fog of the impersonal, the pedantic, the dull, or the undistinguished. Consider how that power lives in a single famous phrase: "God tempers the wind to the shorn lamb." Even the considerable body of deliberate plagiarisms[2] do nothing but increase our wonder that such a little juggling

[1] Such as Sterne, Sermon XI, vol. VI, "On Enthusiasm", and Locke, *Human Understanding*, Book IV, chap. 19, "Of Enthusiasm".

[2] See Dr John Ferriar's *Illustrations of Sterne* (2nd edn, 1812), *passim*.

should mean so great a transmogrification. Here is a sentence from Bacon's essay on Death:[1]

"Groans and convulsions, and discoloured faces, and friends weeping, and blacks, and obsequies, and the like, show Death terrible."

Sterne takes it, shakes it out a little, alters its rhythm and adds the vivid particularization in which he most reveals his genius, and gives us this wonderful sentence:

"There is no terror, brother Toby, in its looks, but what it borrows from groans and convulsions—and the blowing of noses, and the wiping away of tears with the bottoms of curtains in a dying man's room."

Sterne's constructive genius is a more difficult question; it is so much less obvious. We have all been deceived by those squiggly lines which he drew in the sixth book of *Tristram Shandy* to represent the course of his narrative. But any dissatisfaction with the digressive spirit of Sterne's works arises from a misunderstanding of the methods proper to humoristic writing. The conception of plot, which we have continually in mind, owing to our preoccupation with drama and fiction, has nothing to do with the question. It is possible that here again Sterne is indebted

[1] Compare also Jeremy Taylor, *Holy Dying*, chap. iii, sec. 7, 4, for a very similar expression of the same thought.

to Locke, and a contemporary German critic, Rudolf Kassner, has suggested that from the moment when Mr Shandy was so unfeelingly interrupted in the first chapter of *Tristram* by his wife's stupid question about the clock, there is an elaborate play upon Locke's theory of Duration. Sterne certainly seems to have taken hints from this part of the *Essay concerning Human Understanding* (Book II, ch. 14), but the real basis of his method is profounder. To quote Coleridge again, for the last time:

"You must bear in mind, in order to do justice to Rabelais and Sterne, that by right of humoristic universality each part is essentially a whole in itself. Hence the digressive spirit is not mere wantonness, but in fact the very form and vehicle of our genius. The connection, such as was needed, is given by the continuity of the characters."

The characters persist, but the incidents are intermittent. They are finite flashes against an infinite background. This method, which is essential to humour, has a deeper significance for fiction in general. Continuity can be achieved in various ways, but in fiction we have in the past thought too exclusively of the continuity of action, of dramatic interest—in short, we have thought of a *mechanical* continuity. To that kind of continuity we nowadays oppose *psychological* continuity, and

this is achieved either, as notably in the case of
Henry James, by conceiving everything in the
terms of a single consciousness; or else, as in the
case of Marcel Proust, by attempting to get beyond
the system of association and habit which constitutes our normal life and so down to the memory
of that intermittent life of feeling which is the only
reality. Sterne is very modern in this sense. He is
the precursor of all psychological fiction, which
is as though we were to say: of all that is most
significant in modern literature. But his influence
animates more than a literary form. He was the
freest spirit of his century, said Goethe; and
Nietzsche called him the freest writer of all time.
Neither Goethe nor Nietzsche stopped to define
the nature of this freedom, but it seems to have
some analogy to the care-free, ghost-free self-
reliance of the epic hero. In this Sterne's heroes
differ from the typical heroes of the Renaissance.
Hamlet, Don Quixote, Faust—these are great
mythical figures embodying the consciousness of a
race or of an epoch, and in effect thereby tran-
scending their actuality or humanity. But Uncle
Toby and Corporal Trim, and above all Mr
Shandy, are, like Odysseus, at once mythical and
human, and therefore held by us in a peculiar
relation of both grandeur and intimacy.

HAWTHORNE

HAWTHORNE

MR LLOYD MORRIS's recent biography of Hawthorne[1] is a work of genuine merit and deserves the attention which a serious study of Hawthorne's genius should attract. As a biography it belongs to the modern school of 'biography made easy'— it 'runs as lightly as a novel', never halting to make a footnote or support a fact. When it is well done, there is no valid objection to this method; we take the biographer on trust and he presents us, after much labour and deliberation, with a work of art which is, in effect, the outcome of a sound judgment, a skilful control of material, and a scientific probity. It is true that Mr Julian Hawthorne, the son of the novelist, has accused Mr Morris[2] of distorting his father's character in essential particulars; he was robust and 'commonsensical', whereas Mr Morris has made him a very Gentle Fanny, anæmic, morbid and mysterious. But though we must give due weight to a son's impression of his father's personality, we must also remember that nowhere is a man so hidden as in his own family circle, and that the character he wears habitually in other men's eyes is often very

[1] *The Rebellious Puritan. Portrait of Mr Hawthorne.* By Lloyd Morris. London and New York, 1928.
[2] *Saturday Review of Literature*, April 16, 1927.

different from the personality he creates within himself. Mr Morris sees, not a body that moves and speaks in the daily round of life, but a mind whose real dwelling was in the remoter world of fancy and whose speech was certain works of art; and in his attempt to portray that more essential Hawthorne he has our sympathy and a good deal of our admiration.

That Hawthorne was not quite the breezy man of the world of his son's idealization is proved, if need be, by the curious fascination which he exercised on minds so perceptive and so worthy of him as Emerson and Melville. Emerson was impressed by "the painful solitude of the man", yearned for his intimate friendship, but felt a barrier of "unwillingness and caprice". Hawthorne, we know, had a deep scorn for all metaphysical reasoning; he "admired Emerson as a poet of deep beauty and austere tenderness, but sought nothing from him as a philosopher". "For myself", he wrote in *The Old Manse*, "there had been epochs of my life when I, too, might have asked of this prophet the master word that should solve me the riddle of the universe; but now, being happy, I felt as if there were no question to be put." Hawthorne, we feel, was a greater man than Emerson; he held to some truth that gave him the mastery and the inevitable scorn. Herman Melville's cry was deeper: "Whence come you, Hawthorne? By what right do you drink from my flagon of life? And when I put it to my lips—lo, they are yours and not mine. I feel that the Godhead is broken up like the Bread at the Supper, and that we are the pieces. Hence this infinite fraternity of feeling." Hawthorne recoiled from the intensity of Melville's conception of friendship; perhaps, Mr Morris suggests, he did not understand it. "He was incapable of sharing the ecstasies and pangs which their relations yielded to Melville. No doubt he desired neither ecstasies nor pangs. No doubt he desired only peace." Hawthorne had no more liking for mysticism than for metaphysics, but in his rejection of Melville we cannot be equally sure of the rightness of his attitude. It does not go without saying that Hawthorne was the greater man. The greater artist, yes; but Melville's 'divine magnanimities' encompassed far more than Hawthorne's equanimity. In Hawthorne, simple happiness; in Melville, the "profoundest sense of being". "Ineffable socialities are in me. . . . It is a strange feeling—no hopefulness is in it, no despair. Content—that is it; and irresponsibility; but without licentious inclination."

Hawthorne's happiness was perhaps due to nothing more than the simplicity of his life. It is

not fair (to this extent I agree with Mr Julian
Hawthorne) to call him a Puritan, even a rebellious one. In no sense is his art what the psycholo-
gists call a compensation—in no sense a reaction
to environment or education, a working-off of
repressions, a rationalization of fixed ideas. Hawthorne was born with a lively sensibility and that
freedom of mind which best conduces to a
temperate art; and there seems to have been no
attempt to interfere with his natural development.
The only necessities that ever seriously galled him
were economic. He led a strangely secluded life
in his adolescent years, but not stranger than that
of any youth of his temperament born into the
dreary waste of provincial life. His defects (which
have often the appearance of being inhibitions)
are really defects of education—as is most obviously shown in his aversion, later in life, to the
nude statues he found everywhere about him in
Rome. His remark that "man is no longer a naked
animal; his clothes are as natural to him as his
skin, and sculptors have no more right to undress
him than to flay him", strikes us with the force
of its crudity rather than its prudery. It was not
so much a "strange, vague, long-dormant heritage of his strait-laced Puritan ancestry" as a
simple lack of experience. There is surely plenty
of evidence in his writings (in the descriptions of

Zenobia in *The Blithedale Romance*, for example)
to show that the sensuous elements in nature
appealed to him in a normal way. Except that
the Puritan was an integral part of the historical
consciousness which he set himself out to portray,
it is difficult to see how the label ever came to be
applied so freely to Hawthorne. Actually he was
the very antithesis of a Puritan.

It has already been observed that he was no
mystic, and was, if anything, repelled by mysticism. But he was absorbed in something which is
often confused with mysticism—in mystery or
mysteriousness. And this fact is really the key to
his character, if we can arrive at an understanding
of it. There is in *Our Old Home* a passage which
gives us a clue. In itself the passage is a remarkable anticipation of more recent interpretations of
Gothic art. Hawthorne is describing Lichfield
Cathedral:

"To my uninstructed vision, it seemed the
object best worth gazing at in the whole world;
and now, after beholding a great many more,
I remember it with less prodigal admiration only
because others are as magnificent as itself. The
traces remaining in my memory represent it as
airy rather than massive. A multitude of beautiful
shapes appeared to be comprehended within its
single outline; it was a kind of kaleidoscopic

mystery, so rich a variety of aspects did it assume from each altered point of view, through the presentation of a different face, and the rearrangement of its peaks and pinnacles and the three battlemented towers, with the spires that shot heavenward from all three, but one loftier than its fellows. Thus it impressed you at every change, as a newly created structure of the passing moment, in which yet you lovingly recognized the half-vanished structure of the instant before, and felt, moreover, a joyful faith in the indestructible existence of all this cloudlike vicissitude. A Gothic cathedral is surely the most wonderful work which mortal man has yet achieved, so vast, so intricate, and so profoundly simple, with such strange, delightful recesses in its grand figure, so difficult to comprehend within one idea, and yet all so consonant that it ultimately draws the beholder and his universe into its harmony. It is the only thing in the world that is vast enough and rich enough.

"Not that I felt, or was worthy to feel, an unmingled enjoyment in gazing at this wonder. I could not elevate myself to its spiritual height, any more than I could have climbed from the ground to the summit of one of its pinnacles. Ascending but a little way, I continually fell back and lay in a kind of despair, conscious that a flood of uncomprehended beauty was pouring down upon me, of which I could appropriate only the minutest portion. After a hundred years, incalculably as my higher sympathies might be invigorated by so divine an employment, I should still be a gazer from below and at an awful distance, as yet remotely excluded from the interior mystery. But it was something gained, even to have that painful sense of my own limitations, and that half-smothered yearning to soar beyond them."

This sense of an almost giddy vertiginous gulf between human finiteness and the infinity of the Absolute, whether in art or in religion, is the peculiar Northern or Gothic sensibility; and Hawthorne is a very pure representative of it. Nevertheless, he might well feel the painful sense of his own limitations at the sight of a Gothic cathedral, because this sense of the finite and the infinite, and of the infinite in the finite, can only be expressed through the access of an emotional force such as comes from an organized and universal religion. Hawthorne, of course, lacked this support, and fell back on that substitute which has proved a weariness to so many of his readers— symbolism. It is quite extraordinary how large a part this method of expression plays in his work. The greater number of his short stories and the four longer romances are either built round a

symbol or liberally strewn with symbolic illustrations. The frequent introduction of mesmerism
and spiritualism as factors in the plot merely
shows the contagion of contemporary enthu-
siasms, and is a warning of how psycho-analysis in
modern fiction may strike a reader fifty years
hence. But the symbolism of which *The Scarlet
Letter* is the most familiar example cannot so easily
be dismissed. Or, at least, to dismiss it is to dismiss the essential quality of Hawthorne's art.

This quality was well described by Henry James
in that biography of Hawthorne which is such a
significant document in modern criticism, as an
"element of cold and ingenious fantasy", and was
further characterized as 'passionless'. Henry
James did not really appreciate this quality; one
can hardly imagine Henry James appreciating
Spenser and Bunyan, who are its great exempli-
fiers. He remarks, with reference to *The Scarlet
Letter*, that "the absence of a certain something
warm and straightforward, a trifle more grossly
human and vulgarly natural, which one finds in
Adam Blair, will always make Hawthorne's tale
less touching to a large number of even very intelligent readers, than a love story told with the
robust, synthetic pathos which served Lockhart
so well". This was written in 1879, early in
James's own career; and by the irony of events

this is just the sort of criticism which is now being levelled against James's own later work. In fact, though he hardly realized it, James moved in his later years very near to the 'cold and ingenious fantasy', the 'passionless' quality of Hawthorne's tales; for what but allegories, revolving round symbols, are such novels as *The Golden Bowl*, *The Wings of the Dove*, and *The Ivory Tower*? The difference, we would hazard, is merely one of the degree of intelligence involved. Is it possible that the cause determining the form was the same in both cases?

Let us further characterize this form as two-dimensional. It lacks the third dimension of depth, or passion. Hawthorne, who was well aware of the limits of his talent (and this has a great deal to do with his strength) observed of his *Twice-Told Tales* that

"They have the pale tint of flowers that blossomed in too retired a shade—the coolness of a meditative habit, which diffuses itself through the feeling and observation of every sketch. Instead of passion, there is sentiment; and even in what purport to be pictures of actual life, we have allegory, not always so warmly dressed in its habiliments of flesh and blood, as to be taken into the reader's mind without a shiver. Whether from lack of power, or an unconquerable reserve, the

Author's touches have often an effect of tameness; the merriest man can hardly contrive to laugh at his broadest humour; the tenderest woman, one would suppose, will hardly shed warm tears at his deepest pathos. The book, if you would see anything in it, requires to be read in the clear, brown, twilight atmosphere in which it was written; if opened in the sunshine, it is apt to look exceedingly like a volume of blank pages."

And in another place Hawthorne confesses that his native propensities were towards Fairy Land.

All these self-descriptions are meant modestly enough, but they should not be taken as disparagements. Hawthorne's art belongs to that order of fancy which was defined by Coleridge as "a mode of memory emancipated from the order of time and space", and as having "no other counters to play with but fixities and definites". Rather than disparage such works of fantasy, we should respect them as giving free play to the intelligence. Here alone in the world of fiction can the mind range unobstructed by emotion; and here, surely, is the possibility of an art as universal and as indestructible as the 'cloudlike vicissitudes' of Gothic architecture. Its very passionless quality, moreover, assures it of that objectivity which is the aim and distinction of all classical art; and objectivity was a characteristic which Henry James, without these considerations in mind, noted in Hawthorne's writing. It is precisely this objectivity which saves his treatment of Puritanism from any suggestion of inner compulsion.

But we must press this matter farther, to ask how it came about that Hawthorne developed this particular type of art—whether, in other words, there was any compulsion determining the actual quality of his art. This involves us in a very delicate, a very significant, and a very complex problem. It can be briefly stated in words which Henry James used in this connection, and which may stand as a text for the whole debate—"that the flower of art blooms only where the soil is deep, that it takes a great deal of history to produce a little literature, that it needs a complex social machinery to set a writer in motion". Henry James himself took this text very much to heart; it was the problem he himself had to solve, and Hawthorne was the terrible warning he always kept before his eyes. For his definite conclusion was that Hawthorne's art had suffered, and suffered disastrously, irremediably, from the thinness and insipidity of the atmosphere he had been compelled to live in. There is no doubt that in the panic induced by his own situation Henry James tended to depreciate too much the quality of

Hawthorne's work. Above all, he failed to appreciate at its true value what we might call Hawthorne's provincialism. Whatever America of to-day may be, New England of a hundred years ago, in spite of its political independence, was spiritually an outer province of the British Isles. Now a province, though it lacks many of the positive virtues of a metropolis, has some rather negative virtues of its own. It is more confined in its outlook, but tends to send its roots deeper into the soil with which it is, moreover, in directer contact. Much of the best of our literature is essentially provincial—Sterne and the Brontës, and even Wordsworth. But, Henry James would have objected, provincial or not, these authors had a background, whereas in America there is "no State, in the European sense of the word, and indeed barely a specific national name. No sovereign, no court, no personal loyalty, no aristocracy, no church, no clergy, no army, no diplomatic service, no country gentlemen, no palaces, no castles, nor manors, nor old country-houses, nor parsonages, nor thatched cottages nor ivied ruins; no cathedrals, nor abbeys, nor little Norman churches; no great Universities nor public schools—no Oxford, nor Eton, nor Harrow; no literature, no novels, no museums, no pictures, no political society, no sporting class—no Epsom nor Ascot!"

"What was left?" cried Henry James. "Why, simply the whole of life", retorted Howells in a review of *Hawthorne*. James's own answer was that "the American knows that a good deal remains; what it is that remains—that is his secret, his joke, as one may say. It would be cruel, in this terrible denudation, to deny him the consolation of his national gift, that 'American humour' of which of late years we have heard so much".

This is altogether too scornful. It is true that this same 'humour' is still the most trying feature of American writing. Facetiousness is the greatest blemish on Hawthorne's style; it is almost everywhere, and but for its presence Hawthorne would rank with a select company of four or five of our purest writers. An essay like *The Old Manse*, descriptive writing such as is found in *Our Old Home* (surely the best book on England ever written by an American), and, occasionally, intense nervous narrative such as he gives us in *The Scarlet Letter* and *The Blithedale Romance*—these cannot be matched by anything visibly dependent on Eton or Ascot. I will quote two examples:

"He spoke languidly, and only those few words, like a watch with an inelastic spring, that just ticks a moment or two, and stops again. He seemed a very forlorn old man. In the wantonness of youth, strength, and comfortable condition—making my prey of people's individualities, as my custom was—I tried to identify my mind with the old fellow's, and take his view of the world, as if looking through a smoke-blackened glass at the sun. It robbed the landscape of all its life. Those pleasantly swelling slopes of our farm, descending towards the wide meadows, through which sluggishly circled the brimful tide of the Charles, bathing the long sedges on its hither and further shores; the broad sunny gleam over the winding water; that peculiar picturesqueness of the scene where capes and headlands put themselves boldly forth upon the perfect level of the meadow, as into a green lake, with inlets between the promontories; the shadowy woodland, with twinkling showers of light falling into its depths; the sultry heat-vapour, which rose everywhere like incense, and in which my soul delighted, as indicating so rich a fervour in the passionate day, and in the earth that was burning with its love;— I beheld all these things as through old Moodie's eyes. When my eyes are dimmer than they have yet come to be, I will go thither again, and see if I did not catch the tone of his mind aright, and if the cold and lifeless tint of his perceptions be not then repeated in my own."

This shows very exact observation, and a careful, conscious use of words, a subtle sense of rhythm. In the second passage, also from *The Blithedale Romance*, we have the same objectivity applied to a narrative of action:

"We floated past the stump. Silas Foster plied his rake manfully, poking it as far as he could into the water, and immersing the whole length of his arm besides. Hollingsworth at first sat motionless, with the hooked pole elevated in the air. But, by and by, with a nervous and jerky movement, he began to plunge it into the blackness that upbore us, setting his teeth, and making precisely such thrusts, methought, as if he were stabbing at a deadly enemy. I bent over the side of the boat. So obscure, however, so awfully mysterious, was that dark stream, that—and the thought made me shiver like a leaf—I might as well have tried to look into the enigma of the eternal world, to discover what had become of Zenobia's soul, as into the river's depths, to find her body. And there, perhaps, she lay, with her face upward, while the shadow of the boat, and my own pale face peering downward, passed slowly betwixt her and the sky!

"Once, twice, thrice, I paddled the boat up stream, and again suffered it to glide, with the river's slow, funereal motion, downward. Silas Foster had raked up a large mass of stuff, which, as it came towards the surface, looked somewhat like a flowing garment, but proved to be a monstrous tuft of water-weeds. Hollingsworth, with a gigantic effort, upheaved a sunken log. When once free of the bottom, it rose partly out of the water—all weedy and slimy, a devilish-looking object, which the moon had not shone upon for half a hundred years—then plunged again, and sullenly returned to its old resting-place, for the remnant of the century."

But it would be impossible to quote a line further, because facetiousness, in the shape of Silas Foster, stalks all through this otherwise magnificent chapter. Perhaps it would have been juster to quote that other midnight scene, from *The Scarlet Letter*, where Dimmesdale mounts the scaffold where Hester had suffered ignominy; for in that scene Hawthorne's descriptive powers reach an intensity he never equalled elsewhere. But then this scene dissolves into supernatural manifestations of symbolic import which, in their context, have an effect of triviality or irrelevance. It is but another aspect, the serious aspect, of the phenomenon of oblique reference. Whether as humour or as allegory, this phenomenon is the same in all American writers: they walk all round the circumference of a subject and imagine they have been at the centre. Was this not the very quality which Henry James brought with him to Europe and instead of surrendering, merely transmuted into intellectual forms? That, at any rate, is the superficial aspect of his genius.

This phenomenon, however, is merely a question of style. On the question of substance I must hark back to Hawthorne's provincialism, and insist that here was a positive colour, a depth, a density—something of an integrity worth cultivating. It was a tender growth, but how vivid! We might with pleasure turn oftener to the literary charm, the historical interest, the delicate fantasy with which Hawthorne evokes the New England scene, the New England past, the New England character. It is all so authentic; and if in his devotion to it Hawthorne sacrificed the finer graces of ancient culture and the surer power of established tradition, who shall say what the alternative would have cost in moral questionings —the alternative being, as Henry James was to demonstrate, expatriation? It is perhaps not a general question at all—not a question about which the critic has a right to generalize. We can only observe the dilemma, observe that Hawthorne and Henry James avoided it in different ways, and wonder whether a gain in æsthetic values is full compensation for a loss in moral virtue. That there was a third, and a desperate, solution is proved by the case of Poe, who impaled himself on the horns of the dilemma. He could neither accept for good or ill the provincialism he lived among, nor make the necessary effort to escape from it.

This quality in Hawthorne which I have described as provincialism—his particular atmosphere or essence—and the beautiful prose in which it finds expression—these would not in themselves have sufficed to give Hawthorne the high position he occupies in English literature. The heart also was involved. In his Preface to *The House of the Seven Gables* (Hawthorne's prefaces are as important as Henry James's) he once again shows us that he knew all the time what he was about:

"When a writer calls his work a Romance, it need hardly be observed that he wishes to claim a certain latitude, both as to its fashion and material, which he would not have felt himself entitled to assume, had he professed to be writing a Novel. The latter form of composition is presumed to aim at a very minute fidelity, not merely to the possible, but to the probable and ordinary course of man's experience. The former—while, as a work of art, it must rigidly subject itself to laws, and while it sins unpardonably so far as it may swerve aside from the truth of the human heart—has fairly a right to present that truth under circumstances, to a great extent, of the writer's own choosing or creation."

"The truth of the human heart" is perhaps what Howells meant by the whole of human life. It is a sentimental phrase, of course, and Henry James might have argued that the heart can be as impoverished as the body or the mind by a waste environment. Perhaps they can, in an abstract and very evolutionary sense. But it would be obvious nonsense to deny to the New Englander of the nineteenth century, above all to one of such refined sensibilities as Hawthorne, the fullest range of human emotions. And where there are emotions there can be tragedy, and all the forms of literature leading up to tragedy. No one has seriously contended that the inhabitants of America are without original sin—if we may assume the validity of that very necessary dogma; and where there is original sin there also is an original sense of values; and art, especially the art of the novelist, is the working out of such a sense of values. From this point of view two clauses of Henry James's text prove false; neither a deep soil nor a long history is a condition essential for art; and the remaining clause, that it needs a complex social machinery to set a writer in motion, is merely a relative condition. Hawthorne was obviously set in motion, so presumably the simple machinery of New England society was adequate in that sense; and though lack of encouragement and lack of

appreciation may finally defeat the strongest
creative impulse, this impulse in itself is a sub-
jective phenomenon. In so far as art is original
(and that is the last essential test of art), it is innate, and independent of social categories. It is
only the socialization of art—the process by means
of which the art is made available for the community through structures like the epic, the drama
and the novel—it is only this process which suffers
from the absence of a tradition. The poet in that
case is apt to write for himself, or for some ideal
futurity, and to be so much the less universal.

Hawthorne, however, wrote for the New England society of his time, and his art is admirably
proportioned to the nature of this community. It
was, above all, a very self-conscious community.
It took itself very seriously—not only in the sense
that it deliberately cultivated its newly founded
nationality and was already on the lookout for
national heroes and national poets, but also in
the sense that it tried very hard to behave itself
in the eyes of the world. It was preoccupied
especially with moral problems; and in making
these the concern of his writing, Hawthorne was
consciously or unconsciously taking advantage of
whatever virtue of depth there was in the immature society around him. The Puritan conscience
might at first glance seem an unpromising subject

for the delicate visionary that Hawthorne in his early tales had shown himself to be; but his gift of objectivity enabled him to play lightly with the heaviest of materials. "He continued", as Henry James expressed it, "by an exquisite process best known to himself, to transmute this heavy moral burden into the very substance of the imagination, to make it evaporate in the light and charming fumes of artistic production."[1] Henry James then

[1] In this connection it is interesting to compare a short story in *Twice-Told Tales* called "The Minister's Black Veil" with *The Scarlet Letter*. The theme is the same in both cases. But in "The Minister's Black Veil" the hidden remorse of the Rev. Mr Hooper is merely symbolized in the black veil which he wears over his face, and the nature of his remorse is never known; the story remains strictly allegorical. In *The Scarlet Letter*, however, we are very soon made aware of the nature of the Rev. Mr Dimmesdale's remorse, and though we never revel in the modern manner in the details out of which the tragic situation arises, the tragedy itself is worked out on the plane of reality. The fantasy which is the predominant quality of the short tales is in the longer romances reduced to a very subordinate place, and is even then to be regretted. So great is the difference between these two phases of Hawthorne's work that we begin to wonder whether he was subject to some decisive influence at the time he wrote *The Scarlet Letter* (1850). That particular kind of intensity was then rare enough, but manifest in two novels published from a Yorkshire parsonage in 1847. The great similarity between the characters of Chillingworth and Heathcliff would support a suggestion that Hawthorne was inspired in some degree by *Wuthering Heights*; and later we find a confession scene in *The Marble Faun* (1860) closely duplicating a similar scene in *Villette* (1852). Such influences are inevitable, and in writers of independent genius such as Hawthorne they are all to the good, opening out veins which would otherwise remain buried. In any case, such influences are not fruitful unless there is a prior aptitude in the author influenced.

174

goes on to define very exactly the nature of this transmutation:

"Nothing is more curious and interesting than this almost exclusively *imported* character of the sense of sin in Hawthorne's mind; it seems to exist there merely for an artistic or literary purpose. He had ample cognizance of the Puritan conscience; it was his natural heritage; it was reproduced in him; looking into his soul, he found it there. But his relation to it was only, as one may say, intellectual; it was not moral and theological. He played with it and used it as a pigment; he treated it, as the metaphysicians say, objectively. He was not discomposed, disturbed, haunted by it, in the manner of its usual and regular victims, who had not the little postern door of fancy to slip through, to the other side of the wall. It was, indeed, to his imaginative vision, the great fact of man's nature; the light element that had been mingled with his own composition always clung to this rugged prominence of moral responsibility, like the mist that hovers about the mountain. It was a necessary condition for a man of Hawthorne's stock that if his imagination should take licence to amuse itself, it should at least select this grim precinct of the Puritan morality for its play-ground."

This is so truly expressed that it leaves little

more to be said. But Hawthorne's example is one
of very wide significance, and one that can benefit
a generation which is singularly confused on the
subject of the relationship of morality to art. Hawthorne was a 'pure' artist in the modern sense—
as 'pure' as Poe or Landor, Flaubert or Mallarmé.
And yet he was preoccupied with moral problems
—as, to a great extent, was Flaubert also. The
distinction is, of course, that he did not desire a
solution of them—not a solution, at any rate, on
the moral plane. His scorn of the self-concen-
trated philanthropist, and of the meddler in other
people's affairs generally, is evident everywhere—
but especially in *The Blithedale Romance*, which
might have been written for the express purpose
of making this attitude clear. The only agent he
employed in his moral dramas was the conscience;
and all his romances might be described as studies
in remorse, which is conscience accusing itself.
The extraordinary thing, above all in *The Scarlet
Letter*, is the degree of intensity with which the
theme is invested. Indeed, that is the extraordinary thing about Hawthorne altogether, and
the one factor which more than any other inclines
us to rank him as a major artist—the capacity,
that is, which he has for putting an emotional
emphasis into subjects so dispassionately conceived. The resulting art is 'classical', but it is

reached by the reverse of the normal classical procedure of putting a rational curb on to subjects
emotionally conceived. The subjects are indeed
'grim', but the imagination has thrown over them
its own peculiar radiance and glory.

BAGEHOT

BAGEHOT

THE gravest danger in the approach to a critical appreciation of a Mid-Victorian figure lies in a certain deceptive normality which they one and all seem to possess. We think of the age in general as a very stolid one, and we are apt to imagine that its representatives were wholly immobile beneath their frock-coats and florid whiskers. Their works present a certain orderly appearance—are solid, serious and painstaking; and if they do venture upon vain questionings, they do so always with an air of maturity and decorum. Bagehot is, perhaps, a prime representative of this order in the public mind; but in this case, as perhaps in others, the popular conception is singularly false. In another age, and with a different environment, he might have given us cause to rank him as a typical genius and to seek for him all the psychological attributes of genius. That, in any case, he differed from our usual conception of a picturesque genius, such as Blake or Shelley, is not to be denied; to range him with Coleridge and Arnold might cause surprise—but, nevertheless, it is to comparisons of such a nature that we shall be driven. And it is not merely a question of social habit; the name of Coleridge is there to guard against that assumption. It is rather a question of mental faculties, and a more useful line of separation may be drawn between the active or practical genius and the passive or speculative genius. It is a distinction to which Bagehot himself contributed some incisive strokes:

"Certain minds, the moment we think of them, suggest to us the ideas of symmetry and proportion. Plato's name, for example, calls up at once the impression of something ordered, measured, and settled; it is the exact contrary of everything eccentric, immature, or undeveloped. The opinions of such a mind are often erroneous, and some of them may, from change of time, of intellectual *data*, or from chance, seem not to be quite worthy of it; but the mode in which those opinions are expressed, and (as far as we can make it out) the mode in which they are framed, affect us, as we have said, with a sensation of symmetricalness. . . . We may lay it down as the condition of a regular or symmetrical genius, that it should have the exact combination of powers suited to graceful and easy success in an exercise of mind great enough to task the whole intellectual nature.

"On the other hand, men of irregular or unsymmetrical genius are eminent for some one or some few peculiarities of mind, have possibly special defects on other sides of their intellectual nature, at any rate want what the scientific men of the present day would call the *definite proportion* of faculties and qualities suited to the exact work they have in hand."

It may seem at first sight that Bagehot is here making a distinction of externals, that we of to-day, with our psychological methods at hand, can make a finer and profounder analysis. But in further explanation of his meaning Bagehot has a passage which shows the presence of a psychological insight far ahead of the experimental researches of his time. To this characteristic of his we must return, but first let us proceed with the distinction:

"Possibly it may be laid down that one of two elements is essential to a symmetrical mind. It is evident that such a mind must either apply itself to that which is theoretical or that which is practical, to the world of abstraction or to the world of objects and realities. In the former case the deductive understanding, which masters first principles, and makes deductions from them, the thin ether of the intellect—the 'mind itself by itself'—must evidently assume a great prominence. To attempt to comprehend principles without it is to try to swim without arms, or to fly without wings. Accordingly, in the mind of Plato, and in others like him, the abstract and deducing understanding fills a great place; the imagination seems a kind of eye to descry its *data*; the artistic instinct an arranging impulse, which sets in order its inferences and conclusions. On the other hand, if a symmetrical mind busy itself with the active side of human life, with the world of concrete men and real things, its principal quality will be a practical sagacity, which forms with ease a distinct view and just appreciation of all the mingled objects that the world presents—which allots to each its own place, and its intrinsic and appropriate rank."

Bagehot then gives Chaucer as an example of this second type of regular genius, and then concludes:

"Eminence in one or other of these marking faculties—either in the deductive abstract intellect or the practical seeing sagacity—seems essential to the mental constitution of a symmetrical genius, at least in man. There are, after all, but two principal all-important spheres in human life —thought and action; and we can hardly conceive of a masculine mind symmetrically developed which did not evince its symmetry by an evident perfection in one or other of those pursuits, which did not leave the trace of its distinct reflection upon the one, or its large insight upon the other of them."

These are distinctions which in modern psychology have come to assume a normative character;

and a work like Jung's *Psychological Types* is largely
an expansion of the same kind of fundamental
division here made explicit by Bagehot.

These distinctions are, of course, abstractions;
and though Plato and Chaucer may serve as more
or less precise types, our definitions tend to break
down before a test case like Shakespeare. We can,
indeed, call his genius irregular, though it be an
irregularity due to the excess of certain faculties;
or we can boldly say that he is of the type of
'practical seeing sagacity' rather than of 'deductive abstract intellect'. But the truth is rather
that the character of all men, of whatever degree
of genius, is determined not by the exclusive
existence of one or the other of these traits, but
rather by its merely relative predominance; and
certain peculiarly elusive types, possessed of both
tendencies in equal power, seem to hover between
their alternating predominance.

Bagehot himself was of the regular type, though
certain circumstances of his life seem to have pre-
disposed him to a sensitive awareness of opposing
qualities. He was born just over a century ago at
Langport, in Somerset, and came of an old and
landed family more recently established as local
bankers. Perhaps the only abnormal fact of his
early life was the difference of religion between
his parents. His father was by birth and tradition

a Unitarian; his mother, despite her marriage, retained her strong faith in the Established Church. We have to read a little between the lines of Mrs Russell Barrington's *Life of Bagehot*, but it is fairly obvious that a strong attachment, none the less strong for being partially unconscious, existed between mother and son; and there was perhaps a compensating lack of sympathy between son and father. The first important outcome of this disposition of religious forces was that Bagehot was debarred from Oxford by his father's rigid objection to doctrinal tests; he went to University College, London, instead, and the results of this step were far-reaching. Bagehot never seems to have regretted Oxford; nor need we, for the freshness and fairness which strike us as distinguishing him among his contemporaries could not have escaped the retrograde influences then and there at work. It so happened that, instead of these influences working on his mind and imagination through the direct example of Newman, they came to him as the melancholy wreckage of the mind that was Arthur Clough. But that is to anticipate a little.

While still at Bristol College, where he went to school, Bagehot had come under the influence of Dr Prichard, a famous ethnologist, and the learned circle of which he was the centre. Bage-

hot's mind was then given a scientific bias which
it never lost; and when he went eventually to
University College his main interests became
mathematical and philosophical. He took his
degree in 1847, and then went into lodgings with
the purpose of pursuing his studies in philosophy
for the M.A. degree. It is at this period that we
get the fullest insight into his essential character.
His mother suffered from fits of insanity: and this
tragic circumstance, more than anything else,
determined his character and career. An un-
broken persistence of comfortable affection might
have resulted in a pedestrian and unquestioning
intellect; but at the critical stage of his mental
development, Bagehot's whole emotional existence was shaken by this dreadful fact. He then
became endowed with a sensitiveness which, combined with his natural intellectuality, determined
his particular quality. At the age of twenty-one
he went through a phase of morbidity and melancholy for which he found the exact description in
a passage from Keats's Preface to *Endymion*: "The
imagination of a boy is healthy, and the mature
imagination of a man is healthy; but there is a
space of life between, in which the soul is in a
ferment, the character undecided, the way of life
uncertain, the ambition thick-sighted." He quoted
this passage in his essay on Hartley Coleridge,

and there is little doubt that his own experience had confirmed its truth. It was at this period that the potential influences of his time thickly beset him. He seems to have retreated from Newman for curious and characteristically subtle reasons. He thought that Newman was deficient in self-consciousness, and therefore comparatively deficient in aspiration, in the sense of being but little occupied with the future state of his own mind. He accused him of a want of precise moral convictions: the over-activity and restlessness of his mind resulted, to Bagehot's view, in a great facility of analysing to a certain extent, but also in a "great disinclination (almost an inability) to analyse further". And Bagehot adds, in the letter from which we are quoting:

"To finish about Newman, I do not think his want of self-consciousness can be the reason for his wanting precise moral convictions. Arnold, who was not self-conscious at all scarcely, had very precise notions of duty. I think in Newman's case the reason is that his intellect is more subtle than his sense in discriminating: he can conceive finer shades of feeling and motive than his conscience will confidently estimate."

And then came the influence of Clough. Bagehot took the gold medal in Intellectual and Moral Philosophy with his Master's degree in 1848, but he emerged with broken health. In the same year Clough was made Principal of University Hall, which had been established as a hall of residence in connection with University College largely through Bagehot's efforts. During the following two years Bagehot and Clough saw a good deal of each other; and Richard Holt Hutton, who was Bagehot's greatest friend at this time, has recorded his opinion that Clough was "the man who had, I think, a greater intellectual fascination for Walter Bagehot than any of his contemporaries". Clough possessed, and was completely possessed by, that subtle scepticism which was only one component of Bagehot's constitution. Bagehot had, besides, a 'secret vigour' which carried him beyond scepticism: he accepted, in a robust and ready fashion, an irrational fund of faith. This is, of course, the crucial fact about Bagehot's intelligence; according to our own beliefs and temperaments we accept it as the quality that gives to his work all its sanity and symmetry, or we regret that a mind so well endowed with talent should have voluntarily resigned all enquiry into the fundamental questions of philosophy. Our standards are involved: With what scale shall we measure this man? The man himself remains the same.

Bagehot realized all this, and in his essay on

his friend's poems, published after Clough's death in 1861, he reviews not only the fate to which Clough succumbed but also the fate which he, Bagehot, had escaped. He traced the animating cause to the teaching of Dr Arnold. Clough "had by nature, probably, an exceedingly real mind, in the good sense of that expression and the bad sense. The actual visible world as it was, and he saw it, exercised over him a compulsory influence". But "he could not dissolve the world into credible ideas and then believe those ideas, as many poets have done. He could not catch up a creed, as ordinary men do. He had a *straining*, inquisitive, critical mind; he scrutinized every idea before he took it in: he did not allow the moral forces of life to act as they should; he was not content to gain a belief 'by going on living'".

And Bagehot proceeds to show that for such a mind Arnold's teaching was of the worst possible sort:

"He was one of Arnold's favourite pupils because he gave heed so much to Arnold's teaching; and exactly because he gave heed to it was it bad for him. He required quite another sort of teaching: to be told to take things easily; not to try to be wise overmuch; to be 'something beside critical'; to go on living quietly and obviously and see what truth would come to him. Mr Clough

189

had to his latest years what may be noticed in others of Arnold's disciples—a fatigued way of looking at great subjects. It seemed as if he had been put into them before his time, had seen through them, heard all which could be said about them, had been bored by them, and had come to want something else."

A mind thus 'demoralized' was, as Bagehot saw it, exposed to a still worse danger: the Oxford of Newman:

"The doctrinal teaching which Arnold impressed on the youth about him was one personal to Arnold himself, which arose out of the peculiarities of his own character, which can only be explained by them. As soon as an inquisitive mind was thrown into a new intellectual atmosphere, and was obliged to naturalize itself in it, to consider the creed it had learned with reference to the facts which it encountered and met, much of that creed must fade away."

Arnold flattered himself, said Bagehot, that he was a principal opponent of Newman; but he was rather a principal fellow-labourer, and by removing 'the happy apathy' of the common English boy, Arnold was but anxiously preparing the very soil for Newman's unsettling fervour. The way was open for all those subtle questionings which, as Bagehot held in that letter of fifteen years earlier from which we have quoted, never end in certainty or security of mind.

This digression on Clough's fate would not be justified if it did not illustrate so admirably the emotional aspects of Bagehot's own character. He has been accused of hardness, of mere intellectuality, but in truth, as his friend Hutton said, he had "the visionary nature to which the commonest things often seemed the most marvellous, and the marvellous things the most intrinsically probable". For this reason he avoided the obvious outlet for his energies. He wrote of the Whig critics (Jeffrey and the early Edinburgh reviewers):

"Their tendency inclining to the quiet footsteps of custom, they like to trace the exact fulfilment of admitted rules, a just accordance with the familiar features of ancient merit. But they are most averse to mysticism. A clear, precise, discriminating intellect shrinks at once from the symbolic, the unbounded, the indefinite. The misfortune is that mysticism is true. There certainly are kinds of truth, borne in as it were instinctively on the human intellect, most influential on the character and the heart, yet hardly capable of stringent statement, difficult to limit by an elaborate definition. Their course is shadowy; the mind seems rather to have seen than to see them, more to feel after than to definitely apprehend them. They commonly involve an infinite element, which cannot, of course, be stated precisely, or else a first principle—an original tendency—of our intellectual constitution, which it is impossible not to feel, and yet which it is hard to extricate in terms and words."

This passage, more than any other in Bagehot's writings, is to be kept in mind in estimating his character. By the kind of interests he affected, and the nature of his upbringing and training, we might have expected a closer sympathy with the Whig point of view. But Bagehot was a Tory of a very definite type—of a type more intellectual than was usual in the nineteenth century. By virtue of his particular kind of scientific conservatism— the conservatism which sees that the only way to preserve a tradition is to prolong it—he belongs to the school of Bolingbroke and Burke. In another aspect he belongs to the school of Sir Walter Scott, and was an appreciator, and even an exemplifier, of the 'Cavalier' character. "The essence of Toryism", he wrote, "is enjoyment." "Over the 'Cavalier' mind this world passes with a thrill of delight; there is an exultation in a daily event, zest in the 'regular thing', joy at an old feast." "A Cavalier is always young. The buoyant life rises before us rich in hope, strong in vigour, irregular in action; men young and ardent, framed in the 'prodigality of nature'; open to every enjoyment, alive to every passion; eager, impulsive; brave without discipline, noble without principle, prizing luxury, despising danger, capable of high sentiment . . ."—this was the ideal he opposed to Macaulay's chill defect of sympathy, to Clarendon, decorous and grim, and to Hume, "a saving, calculating north-countryman—fat, impassive—who lived on eightpence a day".

Undoubtedly in this matter Bagehot reverted to something fundamental in the English temperament—to something which was Chaucer's and Shakespeare's and Ben Jonson's, but which later became crushed by the multiplication of a severer cast of mind. It is just at this point that we must be careful to distinguish between the subtle and the 'plain' aspects of Bagehot's intelligence. His conservatism was not an outcome of his subtlety but a foil to it; it was, like his religion, an accepted tradition which he might use as a resting-place and a fund of strength but never submit to the refining anxiety of his mind. Some things are too great and simple for that process; hence that sense of poise and equanimity which was his achieved possession. And so his conservatism was the conservatism of simple acceptance, not of fear. The latter type, so prevalent again

to-day, he has analysed in a masterly passage on
the polity of Lord Eldon. He does not fail to
define another type of conservatism to which he
had naturally been inclined, but the limitations
of which he did not hesitate to expose. The type
is still with us, so that the reader can readily test
the acuteness of his description of it:

"There was another cause beside fear which then
inclined, and which in similar times of mis-
cellaneous revolution will ever incline, subtle
rather than creative intellects to a narrow conservatism. Such intellects require an exact creed;
they want to be able clearly to distinguish themselves from those around them, to tell to each man
where they differ and why they differ; they cannot make assumptions; they cannot, like the
merely practical man, be content with rough and
obvious axioms; they require a *theory*. Such a want
it is difficult to satisfy in an age of confusion and
tumult, when old habits are shaken, old views
overthrown, ancient assumptions rudely ques-
tioned, ancient inferences utterly denied, when
each man has a different view from his neighbour,
when an intellectual change has set father and son
at variance, when a man's own household are the
special foes of his favourite and self-adopted creed.
A bold and original mind breaks through these
vexations, and forms for itself a theory satisfactory

to its notions, and sufficient for its wants. A weak mind yields a passive obedience to those among whom it is thrown. But a mind which is searching without being creative, which is accurate and logical enough to see defects, without being combinative or inventive enough to provide remedies —which, in the old language, is discriminative rather than discursive—is wholly unable, out of the medley of new suggestions, to provide itself with an adequate belief; and it naturally falls back on the *status quo*."

A discernment so original as this is evidence in Bagehot himself of a creative intelligence. To share to the extent of understanding "the subtlest quintessence of the most restless and refining abstraction" of Hume or Montaigne, and yet to avoid the easy reaction into which they fell—"the stupidest, crudest acquiescence in the concrete and present world"—such was Bagehot's achievement. His promise was greater. It almost seems as if he came near to defining the specific problem of modern thought, and even possibly had the equipment for the necessary structure of a modern theology. Or was it merely another case of watertight compartments? We do not know, and his most direct statement on such questions, an essay on 'The Ignorance of Man', does not go beyond the affirmation of revelation.

There are still one or two facts to record which bear on the development of Bagehot's character. After taking his final degree, it was decided that he should study law; and this he set himself to do. In due course he was called to the Bar, but he immediately gave up the profession and returned home to Langport, on the solicitations of his mother. He then entered the family business, and thenceforth his life is settled. It should only be noted that the previous year (1851) he had fled to Paris to rid himself of mental depression, and there had the luck to fall in with a revolution. The immediate outcome was a series of letters on the *Coup d'État*, in which he first revealed to the world that he could write "quick sentences [as Woodrow Wilson has called them] of political analysis which were fit to serve both as history and as prophecy". These letters are remarkable for a cynicism to which he was not so much addicted at a later period, but from a literary point of view we can afford to neglect them in favour of the series of critical essays which he began to write as soon as he was settled in his father's counting-house. He was then twenty-six and he had six clear years before him; in that period he wrote nearly all, and certainly most of his best, literary criticism. In 1858 he was married. His father-in-law was James Wilson, Financial Secretary to the

Treasury and proprietor of the *Economist*. Bagehot was thrown upon influences which tended to develop his scientific rather than his literary interests, and in an ensuing period of six years he wrote only five literary essays. Then they stop altogether, and on all such topics he remains mute to the time of his death, in 1877.

But meanwhile these other interests had matured; and in 1867 he published *The English Constitution*, and this was followed in 1870 by *Physics and Politics*, and in 1873 by *Lombard Street*. These three books perhaps with most people constitute Bagehot's chief claim to fame. And indeed they are almost unparalleled classics, belonging to a small group of which Sir Henry Maine's *Ancient Law* is the prototype, in which scientific subjects are endowed with literary qualities by sheer perspicuity of style and sustained animation of interest. These works are secure in their own particular sphere; our only complaint is that they have in some measure detracted from the singular interest of Bagehot's literary criticism. This is almost the best of its time, and only the speculative figure of Matthew Arnold prevents us from pronouncing it quite the best. Arnold's criticism was more deliberate; in a sense it was more cultured. It was scarcely more decisive. What Arnold has gained in the suffrage of time, he lost in immediate effect. In Bagehot's words, what he gained in subtlety he lost in boldness. Perhaps Bagehot would have discerned in the Doctor's son all the worst elements that he had found implanted in Clough; but he does not seem to have expressed himself on the subject, though he was a great admirer of Arnold's poems. Arnold, however, was well aware of Bagehot, and already in 1856 had "traced the same hand" in a series of articles in the *National Review*, which articles seemed to him "to be of the very first quality, showing not talent only, but a concern for the *simple truth* which is rare in English literature as it is in English politics and English religion". Perhaps this is evidence of Arnold's defection from his father's teaching ("a fatigued way of looking at great subjects"); at any rate, it shows a just estimate of the essential quality of Bagehot's criticism, and there is really little else to say about it, except to show the manner of it. This is nowhere so admirably evident as in the estimates he gives of some of his contemporaries. This is always the severest test of a critic, and if we can still read this part of his criticism with interest, we need have no fear for the rest. There is no nineteenth-century critic, Coleridge and Arnold not excepted, who comes out of such a test so admirably as Bagehot. His essays on two such diverse subjects as Dickens and Clough are not only the first but also the last words on these themes. This is a large claim for such a subject as Dickens, who has been the recipient of so much criticism—but how much of it is really criticism? How much of it is not rather the acceptance of a popular estimate and a rationalization of this estimate? If Bagehot made a mistake, it was to imagine that the popularity was impermanent; but his mistake saved him from the inhibitions that have affected later critics, and he had no hesitation in exposing "the natural fate of an unequal mind employing itself on a vast and various subject".

At the base of all Bagehot's criticism was a certain theory of imagination. He held that "the materials for the creative faculty must be provided by the receptive faculty. Before a man can imagine what will seem to be realities, he must be familiar with what are the realities". But, as he wrote in his essay on Shakespeare, "To a great experience one thing is essential, an experiencing nature". In these two observations Bagehot came nearer to an understanding of the process of literary inspiration than any other critic, with the possible exception of Coleridge. He realized that an imagination which does not build on experience is a baseless fabric; and though this is not an original view, it is one that is often forgotten. His further corollary, that there is no real experience without an experiencing nature, embodies a profounder truth; but this he illustrates rather than explains. Goethe, for example, is contrasted with Shakespeare, and Macaulay with Scott. He does not accuse Goethe and Scott of a lack of imagination—who would?—but he points in the former case "to the tone of his character and the habits of his mind. He moved hither and thither through life, but he was always a man apart. He mixed with unnumbered kinds of men, with Courts and academies, students and women, camps and artists, but everywhere he was with them yet not of them. In every scene he was there, and he made it clear that he was there with reserve and as a stranger. He went there *to experience*".

This unexperiencing nature perhaps amounts to no more than a lack of sympathy, but if it were always recognized that sympathy is a necessary component of experience, criticism would be a briefer and more illuminating science.

It is well to remember Bagehot's insistence on sympathy because, in advancing a further and very distinctive characteristic of his criticism, we are in danger of reverting to that false impression of mere hard intellectuality. "What is not possible", he once wrote, "is to combine the pursuit of pleasure and the enjoyment of comfort with

the characteristic pleasures of a strong mind";
and this was his indictment of the eighteenth
century—through which, however, he recognized
there ran "a tonic of business", of political business. His description of the period as "that in
which men ceased to write for students and had
not yet begun to write for women" has hardly
been bettered. It defines three centuries in a
sentence. But what he did admire in the eighteenth century, and in Gibbon in particular, was
"a masculine tone; a firm strong perspicuous
narrative of matter of fact, a plain argument, a
contempt for everything which distinct definite
people cannot entirely and thoroughly comprehend". And this is the manner of his own writing
and the basis of his conception of style: "The most
perfect books have been written not by those who
thought much of books but by those who thought
little, by those who were under the restraint of a
sensitive talking world, to which books had contributed something and a various eager life the
rest." Bagehot himself came near to this ideal;
he was not merely a critic and economist but also
a banker and politician; not merely the author
of a most penetrative essay on Bishop Butler but
also a good horseman and the owner of a pack of
beagles. If anything was lacking it was the
"sensitive talking world".

These varied interests gave to his mind a universality which is rare in literature but of incomparable value. It may seem, on a superficial view, that Bagehot dissipated his energies over too wide a field; that if he had concentrated on criticism, on politics, or on economics, he might have attained the highest possible reputation in one of these narrower spheres. That would be to mistake the quality of the man and to misjudge the proper value of criticism. The opinion of such a man on one literary topic is worth the life-work of a solitary pedant. This universality, combined with that regularity which we noted earlier in this appreciation, gives him that *centrality* of mind which, on a different scale, he had admired in Béranger: "He puts things together; he refers things to a principle; rather, they group themselves in his intelligence insensibly round a principle. There is nothing *distrait* in his genius; the man has attained to be himself; a cool oneness, a poised personality, pervades him."

Such was the character of Bagehot himself; it omits only his wit and his humour, and these may be left to take care of themselves. Had he lived longer his achievement would have been different: he was still developing. But his niche is enviable as it is: *The English Constitution* has a unique place in our literature, and it is doubtful if any book since Hobbes' *Leviathan* has had so much influence on minds which exercise real power. "Had he lived to apply his method", wrote Lord Bryce, "he might have exercised almost the same kind of influence that Montesquieu exerted in the middle of the eighteenth, and Tocqueville in the earlier part of the nineteenth century; and we feel in him the power of an intellect altogether worthy to be compared even with that of the earlier and greater of those two illustrious men." But it is doubtful if that intellect would ever have returned to pure literature; some psychological inhibition seems to have intervened and reformed his interests. We are reminded of a passage in his essay on Bishop Butler:

"Those who know a place or a person best are not those most likely to describe it best; their knowledge is so familiar that they cannot bring it out in words. A deep, steady, undercurrent of strong feeling is precisely what affects men's highest opinions most, and exactly what prevents men from being able adequately to describe them. In the absence of the delineative faculty, without the power to state their true reasons, minds of this deep and steadfast class are apt to put up with reasons which lie on the surface. They are caught by an appearance of fairness, affect a dry and intellectual tone, endeavour to establish their conclusions without the premises which are necessary—without mention of the grounds on which, in their own minds, they really rest."

Did Bagehot himself come to this pass? Did the final insanity and death of his mother release a psychic source too keen for analysis and analogical probing? Did that mind then affect a dry and intellectual tone without mention—perhaps without awareness—of the motive that animated it? The literary critic can only ask these questions: another science must answer them.

❖

HENRY JAMES

❖

HENRY JAMES

THERE is scarcely a problem in the philosophy of criticism which the work of Henry James does not raise, and by raising it lead us to the possibilities of a solution. But these problems, posed by a master of the indirect method, are only slowly emerging into our positive awareness. In their larger aspects, we can distinguish three of them: they concern the novel itself, its form and features; the moral responsibility of the novelist; and the much wider question of the attitude which the artist must adopt in the particular juncture of events at which we modern Europeans find ourselves. Only one of these problems is at all definitely elaborated in the critical writings of the author himself, and this is the purely technical one. To make ourselves familiar with the evolution of Henry James, from his early impersonal experiments in the sixties right through to the final magnificence of his later period, is to trace the historical development of the art of fiction at its intensest creative point. It is to be carried, as in some wonderful ship that somehow manages to keep pace with the sun, right from the world of *Adam Bede* to the world of *The Golden Bowl*. There are other craft in the water; we are in the wake of the rich and overladen argosy of

Balzac; Meredith runs part of the course with us; and Turgenev is a rather remote sailing-ship which we keep in sight all the way; but there is no doubt that the authentic craft, the only one to steer direct, is the very one we have boarded. The experience must be lived through to be appreciated in all its excitement and variety: the traveller's tale in this particular case can only have an air of specious generalization, the unsatisfying blandness of broad effects, a fatal want of vividness and actuality. But in this respect it suffers with all critical effort; for what is criticism but an abstraction from particulars, a surrogate for actuality, a theory to account for facts?

There is a strict sense in which the novels of Henry James are a fund of practical advice. The novice, by the study of them, could learn a hundred useful precepts, and save himself years of unnecessary labour. But the study must be severe, for the perfection is often so complete that we look in vain for any marks of the mould from which it was cast. The surface quality of the work has been a first and final consideration; for 'surface', as we shall see, bears a vital relation to the content and character of the author's wider mission—and we may as well note at once that 'mission' is not a word to be afraid of in this connection. But the 'surface' has its own ob jective qualities; and many of Henry James's precepts are universal enough in their application. Their particular significance must be found in the particular emphasis they get among all the other qualities of his style and method. They are most effectual when they have a disciplinary urgency. The avoided vices are fluidity and discursiveness— "the terrible fluidity of self-revelation" and the discursiveness into which the art of fiction so easily and inevitably falls in irresponsible hands. In a less personal reference Henry James could be vaguer in his requirements:

"The good health of an art which undertakes so immediately to reproduce life must demand that it be perfectly free. The only obligation to which in advance we may hold a novel, without incurring the accusation of being arbitrary, is that it be interesting. That general responsibility rests upon it, but it is the only one I can think of. The ways in which it is at liberty to accomplish this result (of interesting us) strike us as innumerable, and such as can only suffer from being marked out or fenced in by prescription. They are as various as the temperament of man, and they are successful in proportion as they reveal a particular mind, different from others. A novel is, in its broadest definition, a personal, a direct impression of life; that, to begin with, constitutes its value, which is greater or less according to the intensity of the impression."

Here we seem to have no preciser value than interest or intensity. But in actual practice no one could be more relentless in his standard of achievement. For what, to him, did intensity imply but integrity? And once you have let slip this word, in the critical philosophy of Henry James, you have implied a whole organization of values not one of which is less valuable, less indispensable, than the rest. With one decree he has sacrificed all that merely detached descriptive writing which constitutes, one might guess, at least a quarter of the bulk of English fiction. But nothing is now more evident than the fact that this drastic pruning was essential to any further growth; and no critic would now reject the rules worked out by Henry James on this subject, and thus formulated by Professor Edgar in his recent study:[1]

"Localization . . . must never detach itself, either on the one hand from the formative influences of environment on character, or on the other from the formative influences operating from character upon environment. . . . A third prescription, too stringent to impose itself as a law, but still a re-

[1] *Henry James: Man and Author.* By Pelham Edgar. London, 1926.

gulative principle in James's severe practice, sub-
ordinates all descriptions, whether of persons or
of places, to the perceptions of the characters,
and serves, when conscientiously applied, the
salutary purpose of holding the lyrical expansive-
ness of the author in check."

The last requirement is but an aspect of the
general method of indirection for which, above
all authors, Henry James is the sponsor—"that
magnificent and masterly *indirectness* which means
the only dramatic straightness and intensity". But
indirectness is after all only a name for a method,
and it may be asked what purpose can justify a
method admittedly so difficult and involved. The
answer brings us to the greatest essential originality
and modernity of our author.

Henry James perceived, in a real sense which
is distinctive of classic art, and in a sense which
gives us the real sense of the Greek conception of
dramatic unity, that the problem of 'presentation', of 'projection', of the translation of action
into verbal expression, was a problem of time. It
is a question of creating an *illusion* of duration
which shall correspond with an actual *sense* of
duration. The illusion can only be effective if the
strands of interest which we pick up at the beginning of a story are so woven that they duplicate
our consciousness of real events. But conscious-

ness, whether real or induced, is not a simple fact: it is rather a process or state which is only realized upon the completion of some definite rhythm or pattern. In this it differs from awareness, which is an incomplete state of sensibility. We say loosely that we are 'conscious' of pain or pleasure, but it would be better to say that we are 'aware' of them. We become 'conscious' when pain or pleasure is organized into a recognizable unity—when it becomes a sentiment, such as pity or terror. For pity or terror, or love or hate, is a highly organized complex, depending for its duration on its inherent pattern or repetitive rhythm. Still more complex are those organizations of emotions and conscious states which we name personalities, and those too have their dependable rhythm or definite pattern. Now, in order to create personalities and set them in action (which is the object of fiction), it is necessary to repeat, on another plane, an analogous rhythm or pattern.

The discovery, or rediscovery and application to fiction, of this principle was the great technical advance made by Henry James. It is an advance of the very greatest importance: it is not too much to say that upon the making-good of this advance by future novelists the whole art of fiction depends. How Henry James came to make this discovery is a different question, which must be dismissed briefly here. There were two steps: In the first place, his intelligence grasped the nature of the problem to be solved, though perhaps other writers have gone thus far. But then Henry James had the further and abounding grace to perceive that the problem could not be solved formally, æsthetically, or in pure abstraction, but must be *applied* to the actual current of existence. The rhythms could not be invented, but must be caught up from the actual idioms of daily life; and equally the patterns must be outlined in the wider pattern of civilization. The first, or dynamic, aspect of duration is solved on the moral plane; the second, or static, aspect is the aggregation of acts committed on the moral plane, and constitutes the problem implied in our sense of tradition or civilization.

It is difficult to cope with the complexity of interrelations which gather thickly at this point. There is the writer's concern for perfection in his medium, and there is his concern for the truth and actuality of his material. These may be unrelated activities—and indeed are so in most writers, and even, in some, tend to conflict. But in others, and above all in Henry James, there is a further concern that the particular material in hand shall have its particular perfection of medium. The style and method are not only perfect, but also perfectly adapted to the subject-matter. And the complexity does not end there; for over the choice of theme, its development in the dramatic sense, there still hovers the possibility of a further perfection in the formal arrangement or pattern of the action—so admirably illustrated for us in *The Awkward Age*. And further still, all these interrelated perfections can still offer the temptation of still another pattern, a pattern which is the whole glowing perfection of one's philosophy of life—a perfection which, if intelligently sustained, governs with one last implied necessity the formal organization of life—the interrelation, that is to say, of each and every activity.

Some of the implications of a doctrine of perfection are suggested by an illuminating comparison which Professor Edgar draws between Henry James and Racine:

"Perfection is of admittedly various kinds, but even in its most consummate form it is not necessarily the mark of supreme greatness. Narrowly considered, there is more perfection of finish and design in half a dozen of the masterpieces of Racine than in any of Shakespeare's plays, yet we are satisfied to sacrifice something of the harmony of the one for the abundance and energy of the other. Now the perfection that James wrought for and not infrequently achieved is more Racinean

than Shakespearean. Soft flowing contours and
harmonies of line distinguish it—a disciplined
energy, a temperate warmth, and a refinement of
execution that suggest rather deliberation than
spontaneity. In either writer, too, a like fastidiousness prevails, which in the interests of concentrated effect clears the stage of all superfluous
figures and defines strictly the limits within which
the action is permitted to develop. I do not wish
to involve myself in a prolonged comparison of
two writers whose methods exhibit such obvious
affinities, for their dissimilarities would necessitate
as copious a discussion. There is this remark, however, to make, that whereas Racine, who chooses
his themes for their rich human implications,
seems never to concern himself with manipulating
them so as to produce the illusion of reality,
James, on the other hand, selects subjects which
do not appear, save to himself, to hold the promise
of germination, but develops them in accordance
with the strictest logic of life."

'The logic of life' is a remote phrase, for
nothing, in common experience, has so little logic
about it. Life is not an armoured syllogism, but
an elusive growth. Yet there is a logic concerned,
and this is the logic of art or imagination. The
very next sentence in Professor Edgar's book
seems to contradict his phrase; for he says of

Henry James that "it was his theory that the artist is privileged to give the law to life, and to submit her haphazard processes, her waywardness, her profuse extravagance, or even her occasional meagreness, to a control more severe than the discipline she herself imposes". And this, of course, is the truth of the matter: the imagination seizes upon one of the disjointed events of which life for the most part is made up, and develops that event into a fable which has not the casual and occasional aspect of existence but the harmonious autonomy of art. Art, in fiction, is not a true report, but a convincing fable. But the fable is always a deduction from experience; and the word 'develops', a few lines above, hides a process which may rightly be called logical. For when events do not 'happen', as in life, then they must be created in a region of speculation, an aery void where our only guide is an innate sense of their rightness. And 'right' not only in their probability and necessity but in all the other virtues of the Aristotelian canon—in unity, beauty, universality and moral purpose.

The faith of the artist in these matters is that the logic of art will, if persisted in, somehow include the 'logic of life'. The presiding idea will, that is to say, somehow provide for every possible relation and complexity included in its scope. All possible aspects are realized in the round mass of the work; all possible values are compounded within its unity. To the degree of perfection attained by Flaubert (to take his most immediate predecessor in these matters) Henry James added another dimension; and this further dimension made all the difference between failure and success. In an essay on Flaubert Henry James once used a devastating image to evoke the general significance of *L'Éducation Sentimentale*, describing it as "a huge balloon, all of silk pieces strongly sewn together and patiently blown up, but that absolutely refuses to leave the ground". It meant more than it can ever mean to us for a critic of the last generation to be able to discriminate in this fashion between a labour so extensive in scale and so perfect in finish and that labour's lack of any inner volume or enabling medium; because only one who had gone all the way with Flaubert until he had outstripped him and turned to survey him, only one whose mind could rise above the merely empirical elaboration of beauty to an intelligence controlling beauty, only Henry James could designate the falsity, the irony, the lack of any centre of sympathy, in the work of Flaubert:

"Thus it is that as the work of a 'grand écrivain', large, laboured, immensely 'written', with beautiful pages and a general emptiness, with a kind of leak in its stored sadness, moreover, by which its moral dignity escapes—thus it is that Flaubert's ill-starred novel is a curiosity for a literary museum."

'Moral dignity' brings us nearer the burning heart of Henry James's world than any other phrase in the vocabulary of criticism; these two words summarize his significance, and all that is left to the critic is to ease out their concentrated meaning.

Henry James was born with a moral sense; and the first aspect of the significance of the moral problem in his work is nothing but the significance of the problem in his life. He first came to consciousness in a world of strict Puritanism, but only immediately to be plunged into the sensuous life and colour and tone of Mediterranean Europe. As a child and youth he flitted like a winged envoy between the opposed civilizations. A docile mind or a dogmatic might have come to an early decision and stayed irrevocably in one or other sphere. But James had a discriminating mind; he was sensitive to the values of both worlds, and also conscious of the fact that those values were irreconcilable. He did finally make a conscious choice, as we shall see, but the dualism of his appreciative sense gave a lasting tension to his mind. Professor Edgar has observed this same duality:

"In Henry James, and I would speak of both the novelist and the man, there is a curious blending of opposed elements. He would be the most sophisticated of men and writers if he were not so ingenuously naïve, and it may well be this unwonted union of *naïveté* and sophistication that establishes his identity, that gives his character its mould and his work its distinguishing quality."

Puritanism is a private virtue, but a public vice. In the individual it implies a moral constraint whose outcome is probably a finer sense of intellectual and æsthetic discrimination. But in public life Puritanism withers and blasts every finer manifestation of the corporate life; it is fatal to joy and grace, and eventually to religion and art. Professor Edgar says that "the defect of Puritanism is a lack of charity; its merit is that it has a standard of discrimination between right and wrong that resists the easy ebb and flow of occasion and arbitrates between our duties and our desires." This is true, but not searching enough. The standard of discrimination, if it is not to be a meaningless tyranny, must be an individual creation: it must be relative to the individual alone; and Puritanism lacks charity because it presumes to apply the measure of a personal rectitude to other minds and other epochs; what is evolved from a particular set of circumstances is enforced as a universal code.

It is to the personal aspect of Puritanism that Henry James clings desperately; so desperately that his most moving creations, beautiful figures like Milly Theale or Maggie Verver, are embodiments of a fine moral integrity, of conscience in all its infinite reaches and delicate adjustments. And wherever Henry James takes this integrity of character as his theme, there he creates his most enduring impressions. And these impressions are enduring precisely because they have gained in delicate extension, in infinite spiritual ramifications and crystallizations, what they have lost— not lost, but expended—in mere brute force and physical capacity. In this sense it is a perfectly clear issue, fully realized and consciously carried to its conclusions by Henry James. How explicit it is, for example, in his criticism of the 'vulgarity' of d'Annunzio's love scenes, which he ascribes to the weakness of that author's sense of 'values':

"We begin to ask ourselves at an early stage what this queer passion may be in the representation of which the sense of beauty ostensibly finds its richest expression and which is yet attended by nothing else at all—neither duration, nor propagation, nor common kindness, nor common con-

sistency with other relations, common congruity
with the rest of life—to make its importance good.
If beauty is the supreme need so let it be; nothing
is more certain than that we can never get too
much of it if only we get it of the right sort. It is
therefore on this very ground—the ground of its
own sufficiency—that Signor d'Annunzio's in-
vocation of it collapses at our challenge. The
vulgarity comes from the disorder really intro-
duced into values, as I have called them; from the
vitiation suffered—that we should have to record
so mean an accident—by taste, impeccable taste,
itself."

Beauty is the supreme need, and vulgarity, or
ugliness, comes from a disorder of values. But
whose values? Physical passion itself, in the
colours d'Annunzio lends it, is a value. Yes, but
not of the right sort, is the answer we derive from
the quoted criticism. And 'the right sort' is, for
Henry James, the crux of the whole problem. It
is, at any rate, the problem to which he devoted
the whole of his life.

Just as previously we have seen him take the
method of fiction into another depth or dimension
of effect, giving it density and duration and whole-
ness, so now we see him taking the problem of
conduct beyond individual implications and facing
the wider, the vaster, and the more portentous

problem of civilization. Implicit in his discovery that the values of Puritanism are individual, was his discovery that the values which Puritanism does not provide for—does, in effect, so far as it becomes a system or a creed, tend to destroy— were precisely the social values, the values of civilization. And it was with the birth of this consciousness that Henry James entered upon his peculiar destiny.

There has been an attempt to treat the definite decisions and preferences by which Henry James slowly but surely dissociated himself from the country of his origin as so many steps in a spiritual decline. It is felt that by renouncing the crude but incalculable potentialities of American life he displayed a fastidiousness which rejected the rough virtues of rude health for the iridescence of decay. An American critic, Mr Van Wyck Brooks, has even gone so far as to attempt a correlation between this assumed moral decadence and the development of Henry James's style and method. This kind of criticism must, we feel, be condemned on its own evidence: it cannot for a moment be admitted that the later style and method of this author, complex and difficult as they may be, are, on any sound basis of knowledge or clear refinement of sensibility, inferior to the comparatively simpler, but in that measure less characteristic, style and method of the early works. We see rather a style beginning as a careful inference from particular models (there is Hawthorne, and George Eliot, and a temperate Ruskin in it), but slowly emerging into individuality and force until finally it becomes one of the most flexible and most adequate styles in English literature.

The truth is, rather, that a critic like Mr Van Wyck Brooks quite misconceives the true significance of Henry James, and is incapable of appreciating his concept of values. You may, from the virgin soil of a new continent, look upon Europe as a land of dead values and decaying manners; you may think of our civilization as one that has run its course and must inevitably complete a fatal destiny. It is very possible to generalize in such a manner, and it is very fashionable. And there is no need, for the moment, to throw doubt on this facile fatalism, however unscientific and unreasonable it may appear to be. For without involving ourselves in any historical prophecies, we can freely admit the decay of manners and civilization in the modern world. But who realized this more keenly than Henry James himself? And precisely his mission, once he had found himself on solid ground, was the pitiful unmasking of this decay, and the reaffirmation of a few quiet, essential virtues within the fabric of society.

The virtues are quiet and infinitely individual and reticent; but they have a way, when considered, of reverberating to the confines of empires and civilizations. The virtues of Lambert Strether in *The Ambassadors* (to take a simple case), the almost allegorical figures of Mrs Newsome and Madame de Vionnet, and the other cardinal qualities built into the action of the book, all these make for a suspense such as no mere play of characters could secure, but which comes from the sense we have, as we read, of an invisible chorus of fates. More prosaically, we are aware of the conflict, within the exemplary consciousness of Strether, of two civilizations. It would be more exact to say: of civilization and its opposite, barbarism.

In *The Ambassadors* Henry James represented the tragedy of his own life: and a careful study of this book—which he himself regarded as his masterpiece—is a necessary preliminary to any understanding of the significance of his work. But it is doubtful whether this book, or any other of his writings, would countenance as the antithesis of civilization so brutal a term as barbarism. There is the gentler word provincialism, and it is a word he often used—so often that Howells protested against it in a review of Henry James's *Hawthorne*. It is a word rather typical of Henry James, and it indicates an attitude *within* a civilization. Types are seen as conforming, or as simply not conforming, to a single standard. A more dispassionate observer would see the extremes more violently: would see types tending in one direction, towards civilization, or in the opposite direction, towards barbarism. But this is too theoretical a position for Henry James; and the values of civilization are for him fully conditioned by the visual and tactile objects of which it is severally and sensibly constituted. *The Spoils of Poynton* gives us this relation most clearly. But in a letter to Howells—an answer to the protest just referred to—the doctrine is stated in all its naked force:

"I sympathize even less with your protest against the idea that it takes an old civilization to set a novelist in motion—a proposition that seems to me so true as to be a truism. It is on manners, customs, usages, habits, forms, upon all these things matured and established, that a novelist lives—they are the stuff his work is made of; and in saying that in the absence of those 'dreary and worn-out paraphernalia' which I enumerate as being wanting in American society, 'we have simply the whole of human life left,' you beg (to my sense) the question. I should say we had just so much less of it as these same 'paraphernalia' represent, and I think they represent an enormous quantity of it."

Civilization for Henry James meant a perfectly definite historical phenomenon: it meant in general the continuous tradition of culture which Western Europe inherited from the ancient world; it meant more particularly the Renaissance tradition in which we still exist, in however attenuated and debased a fashion. But again it would be a mistake to imagine that Henry James's sense of civilization was historically apprehended; such æsthetic judgments as we find him making are often curiously lacking in all sense of historical perspective; he does not handle the actual spoils of civilization with any very genuine signs of appreciation, and his references to paintings and *objets d'art* are often clumsy enough. Nor do we ever discover that such things played any vital or individual part in his own life. It is all so much a feeling for the general glory, as so beautifully conveyed in that silvery flood of eloquence in which he recovers, in *A Small Boy and Others*, his first impression of the Galerie d'Apollon. His acutest realizations gathered round the spiritual significance of these symbols; and perhaps his preference for the reactions rather than the reagents is after all only his recognition that civilization is a matter of mental condition rather than of vulgar possession—a state of refinement which comes by instinct or inheritance, but never by conveyance.

Civilization was in his view a phenomenon of ever-increasing complexity, and to refuse the effort required to comprehend and develop this complexity was to deny the life of intelligence itself. Of two such denials he was conscious in a sure but intuitive manner. One is represented by the America he deserted, and the other, as well as by anything, by the Russia which confronted him in Tolstoi and Dostoievski. His attitude towards America was, as we have already seen, the animation and action of his whole life and work: his attitude towards Russia was no less real, though it never occupied his attention to the same degree. It was a blind reaction which emerged in an almost violent scorn of the two writers just mentioned—"fluid puddings, though not tasteless, because the amount of their own minds and souls in solution in the broth gives it savour and flavour, thanks to the strong, rank quality of their genius and experience". And in another place he says: "I think it is extremely provincial for a Russian to be very Russian . . . for the simple reason that certain national types are essentially and intrinsically provincial." Perhaps he would have made that overworked label suffice as a connecting-link between his antipathies. Perhaps nowadays we can see stronger and more essential links; such links are being forged by

events, and the process of 'Americanization',
which carries with it all the determinate forces of
materialism and mechanism, nowhere seems so
irresistible as among the comparatively tradition-
less peoples of Russia. Is not the deepest significance of the revolution in Russia to be found in
its renunciation of Europe? Its force and endurance can only be explained by a recognition
of this historical truth: that there has been no
suppression of the national ethos, but rather a
renewal. Russia has retreated to her own fast-
nesses. The political doctrine with which the new
régime is identified, although of European origin,
is one which even its European adherents would
admit to be totally disruptive of the cultural tradition of the West. To one who had solemnly elected
for this tradition there could be no further vacilla-
tion: that election had been too deeply confirmed
by anguish of mind and force of emotion. And
if to-day we wished to take from the world of
literature two antithetical types representing the
dominant and opposite forces of the modern world,
we could not find two so completely significant
as Dostoievski and Henry James. In the one is all
energy, all evil, obscurity and confusion, the
dreadful apocalypse of a conscience that has lost
all civilized sanctions and has no foundations to
its world; and in the other a calm, dominant,

reticent and fastidious intellect, ordering the gathered forces of time to a manifestation of their most enduring glory.